CATCHING THE NEXT WAVE

Leadership Strategies for Turn-Around Congregations

STEVEN J. GOODWIN

CATCHING THE NEXT WAVE
Leadership Strategies for Turn-Around Congregations

Editors: Andrea Lee Schieber, Jill Carroll Lafferty
Illustrations: Marti Naughton
Cover design: Mike Mihelich
Cover photo: PhotoDisc, Inc. copyright © 1998

Developed in cooperation with the Division for Congregational Ministries of the Evangelical Lutheran Church in America, Marta Poling-Goldenne, project manager.

This book has a companion resource, *Catching the Next Wave Workbook: Leadership Strategies for Turn-Around Congregations*, 0-8066-3882-6. Order copies from Augsburg Fortress, 800-328-4648.

Goodwin, Steven J., 1961–
Catching the next wave : leadership strategies for turnaround congregations / Steven J. Goodwin
p. cm.
Includes bibliographical references.
ISBN 0-8066-3881-8 (alk. paper)
1. Church renewal. 2. Christian leadership. 3. Church growth.
I. Title.
BV600.2.G65 1999
250—dc21 99-24095
CIP

The paper used in this publication meets the minimum requirements of the American National Standard for Information Sciences—Permanence of Paper for Printed Library Materials, ANSI Z329.48-1984.

Manufactured in the U.S.A. AF 9-3881

99 00 01 02 03 04 1 2 3 4 5 6 7 8 9 10

Contents

Preface

This book was written out of self-defense. Serving a ninety-four-year-old congregation with a tumultuous history in a rapidly growing urban area (rural becoming urban) near Seattle forced me to wrestle with the issues of vision and mission. I was compelled to master lessons on leadership that I hadn't learned at seminary. I was forced to my knees in prayer because I was in over my head serving as pastor of a congregation in decline. Quickly came the realization that Jesus was the Messiah of the congregation—not me! Even so, I had to develop some skill to be of use in God's divine vision for the flock I was called to shepherd.

It is my prayer that this book will be helpful to many congregations that are struggling with the issue of how to reform a plateaued or declining church. In the spirit of Martin Luther, my forebear in the faith, I hope that God may use this book to enable the church to be always reforming. In an era filled with rapid change, the church cannot stand still.

Special thanks to my gifted wife, Lisa, who encouraged, gently prodded, and believed in me. Her skills acquired long ago as a tutor in the writing lab of Bethel College, St. Paul, Minnesota, proved of continuing use. I also thank my children, Johnny and Gracie, for their patience in understanding that "Daddy has to write now." I pray that my work will inspire them both to achieve for the glory of God beyond that which they think possible. I am indebted to my editor, Andrea Lee Schieber, who was a joy to collaborate with on this project.

Finally, I want to thank the saints of the Evangelical Lutheran Church in America who have taught me what I know about ministry. I am grateful for the love and support I have received from my church. Every time I sat down to write, I asked God to use what I have learned so that it might nourish the church that has so nourished me.

May Christ's church always be reforming!

1 Hallmarks of Congregational Health
Defining Congregational Health

In the beginning God created the heavens and the earth.

Genesis 1:1 RSV

The narthex of Christ Church bustles with energy. Worshipers enthusiastically bring friends and neighbors to see what is happening among this dynamic group of people. Between worship services the building overflows with Christian education classes for children and adults. Throughout the week, no less than Sunday morning, the congregation brims with vitality as it reaches out with the love of Christ through its many social ministries to its community. Even casual observers sense there is something about this congregation that conveys Christ. All would quickly agree that this is a very healthy church.

But just what is it about Christ Church that makes it so healthy, so alive in Jesus Christ? What is it that visitors and members alike feel but find so hard to put into words? What defines a healthy church? With this question we begin our search for answers to turn around plateaued and declining congregations. Only when we have a clear picture of a healthy congregation can we begin the journey of turning things around.

God the creator

God is the creator of all things. Our God is a God of life. Amoebas to albatrosses, turnips to trees, zoophytes to zebras, God has fashioned life as we know it. This life God has so wondrously made exhibits intentional design. Life has purpose, structure, system, and order. Life is a balance of a complex set of variables, the sum total of which eludes human understanding. We see this in part through the beautiful creation story of Genesis 1, where God takes the formless and gives it form and limit. God creates successive layers, each of which interacts with every other created element. And God saw that it was good.

In a similar sense, we also speak of God as the creator of spiritual life. God promises us not only eternal life through our Savior Jesus Christ, but also promises that our present life will be transformed. This revealed truth inspired the apostle Paul to write to the Romans, "Therefore just as one man's trespass led to condemnation for all, so one man's act of righteousness leads to justification and life for all" (Romans 5:18). In chapter 6 Paul continues to argue that through Jesus, new life comes into the present life of the believer. "Therefore we have been buried with him by baptism into death, so that, just as Christ was raised from the dead by the glory of the Father, so we too might walk in newness of life" (Romans 6:4).

God took the formless and breathed life into it. By grace through faith, God is at work creating new life within us. Like its biological counterpart, spiritual life bears God's hallmark characteristics of purpose, structure, system, and order. The church is one among many manifestations of God's creation of life. The church is brought into being by God's word. It exhibits form and limits just as the remainder of creation. God has breathed the Spirit into the church and it too bears God's purpose, structure, system, and order (Acts 2, 6; Romans 12; 1 Corinthians 12). Therefore, we can see that in both the biological and spiritual realms, God has been consistent in the fashioning of life.

Life and health

Yet just what exactly is life? Even biologists, whose calling it is to study life, cannot precisely define it. Despite centuries of research, a definition of life is still elusive. Biologists are able only to describe what life looks like. Life, in a biologist's definition, is characterized by seven hallmarks: organization, growth, movement, transformation (metabolism), sensitivity (biologists use the term "irritability," in other words, reaction to stimuli), adaptation, and reproduction.[1] In attempting to determine the nature of life, we are limited to this broad description of God's majestic creation.

As we observe the life God created, we cannot help but be astonished by the layers of design. We can only marval at this intricate web of life. Built into this complexity is a beautiful balance of countless variables working simultaneously just as God set forth. This balance is what we describe as health.

In seeking a universal definition of health, we encounter the same dilemma we face in outlining what life is. Defining health is rather like defining art or beauty. How do we conceptualize that which is beyond our full intellectual grasp? We can only make feeble attempts to describe the nature of health.

Peter Steinke is a Lutheran pastor and church consultant who has worked with many pastors and congregations in difficulty. Steinke defines health as "wholeness. Health means all the parts are working together to maintain balance. Health means all the parts are interacting to function as a whole. Health is a continuous process, the ongoing interplay of multiple forces and conditions."[2]

A holistic approach to health involves a range of normal. Health is a balance of both macroscopic and microscopic variables in complex interrelationships. It cannot be pinned down with precision, nor can it always be quantified or qualified. There is no universal standard for measuring health. Pronouncing something to be healthy is made all the more difficult because each observer has a unique definition of health.

The closest we can come to a standard definition is to say that health is the dynamic interplay of wondrous layers of interrelationship to accomplish God's purpose and glory. The source of this balance stems from the blueprints used by the Creator of life. To talk about health is, therefore, to point back to God's original intent for life. Health is our expression for the normal functioning of life as God has designed it. Given this we then may ask, What is a healthy congregation? What does it look like? What qualities does it possess? What standards shall we use to declare one congregation healthy and another unhealthy?

Church growth

In the last half of the twentieth century, the church growth movement sought to answer these questions. The church growth movement began with the 1955 publication of Donald McGavran's book, *The Bridges of God.*[3] McGavran's ideas were gleaned through frontline mission experience in India from 1923 to 1954. Upon leaving the mission field he committed his life to careful sociological research on why churches grow. Decades of experience forged his ideas until finally, in the mid-1970s, they exploded onto the ecclesiastical scene. Suddenly, "church growth" was the talk of theologians, pastors, and lay leaders across the world. McGavran's methodology was refined and popularized by his students, most notably C. Peter Wagner, Win Arn, Elmer Towns, and Carl George.

The church growth movement has been used by God to rekindle the church's zeal for evangelism. It offers to renew our attention to disciple making in our own communities and on foreign mission fields. It has provided a long overdue corrective to our era's self-centered focus on congregational members alone. In the words of the late contemporary Christian songwriter Keith Green, the church has "fallen asleep in the light."[4] Church growth has offered us understanding about why churches grow or decline. These insights, taken in their proper context, have invigorated the church.

The church growth movement has also produced strong reactions. Initially, one tended to either love or hate this new emphasis. Rarely has a theological methodology garnered so many devotees and so many ardent opponents as church growth. Those who embrace the church growth movement praise it for restoring to the church its long-lost zeal for the Great Commission (Matthew 28:19-20). Others reject it out of hand, characterizing it as being too numbers oriented, artificial, and narrow.

Elmer Towns, dean of Liberty University and an ardent church growth supporter and theorist, notes the weaknesses of the movement's principles. Towns says, "First, there are exaggerated expectations and claims. Some church growth leaders place such high value in their principles that they claim any church, anywhere, any time, can grow. Second, there are some superficial articles or books. By reducing the whole movement to hunches or practical suggestions, we have become superficial in our own self-opinion. Third, some church growth leaders are so committed to growing the church, they have compromised biblical principles just to get numbers or results. Fourth is 'kingdom building'; some leaders build 'private kingdoms.' "[5] Church growth's shortcomings aside, we must agree theologically that God intends God's kingdom to come. Undoubtedly, this will entail growth. However, the church growth movement's narrow definition of a healthy church must be judged as inadequate.

Church health

In recent years a new movement has appeared on the church's radar screen, a movement that might best be described as "church health." This new emphasis is the convergence of two independent schools of thought. First, prominent thinkers within the church growth movement, such as Robert Logan and Christian Schwarz, are challenging the movement to grow past its awkward adolescence into a broader understanding of church life. Rick Warren, pastor of Saddleback Valley Community Church in Mission Viejo, California, states his belief is that "the key issue for churches in the twenty-first century will be church *health* [Warren's emphasis], not church growth."[6] This broader concept of what the church ought to be is resonating with many who previously tuned out.

Church growth must be reenvisioned as church health. While growth must certainly be acknowledged as one of the characteristics of all living things, it is not the only measure of healthy life in a body. The church health movement promises to broaden the Christian church's understanding of what constitutes a healthy congregation by embracing other characteristics that are essential for life and health.

Christian Schwarz is one such new theorist who seeks to move church growth in this new direction of church health. Schwarz directs our attention to what he terms "natural church development."[7] Schwarz has recently published the largest, most comprehensive study of Christian churches in the world. Surveying more than one thousand congregations of varying denominations across all continents, Schwarz distills eight criteria for healthy congregations. These are: empowering leadership, gift-oriented ministry, passionate spirituality, functional structures, inspiring worship services, holistic small groups, need-oriented evangelism, and loving relationships. Combining biology with sociology, Schwarz offers the church a fuller way to understand its life together.

A second school of thought converging with a reenvisioned church growth movement is represented by theologians and church leaders who never embraced church growth. Conflict, stagnation, paralysis, loss of vision, and factions within the membership are just a few of the manifold problems faced by congregations. The attempt by this school has been to address these obstacles by intertwining family systems theory, conflict management, social psychology, and leadership theory. Peter Steinke has been a leader in this movement seeking to heal the church where it is broken and wounded. In his experience as a pastor and counselor, Steinke sees up close the wounds of congregations.

Steinke's most recent book, *Healthy Congregations: A Systems Approach*, intersects the thought of Schwarz and uses a multidisciplinary approach to craft a new way of thinking about the challenges to the church. Leaning heavily on biological principles of health and family systems theory, Steinke's thought is rapidly winning an audience throughout the church in the United States and Canada.

Hallmarks of health

So how shall we define a healthy congregation? If we return to our earlier discussion of God as the creator of both biological and spiritual life, then we might apply biology's description to the life of healthy congregations.

Organization

Life bears intrinsic organization. DNA has a pattern and is structured in a double helix formation. Cells have nuclei to retain their molecular instructions, mitochondria to provide energy, and a membrane to encapsulate the cell keeping undesired foreign objects out. Animals have organs and organ systems that function interactively.

The church cannot exist without organization any more than the most simple, single-celled organism. Whether it is the basic organization of a house church or the complex structures of Roman Catholicism, the congregation requires clear organizing structures to be truly alive.

Growth

Growth is the second hallmark of life. Growth distinguishes living things from all nonliving things. Even after reaching mature size, living things continue to grow. Even as the organism nears the end of its life cycle, the capacity for growth remains. Cells continue to divide, taking the place of other cells.

The book of Acts most clearly exhibits this facet of the life of the church of Jesus Christ. The early church grew numerically, yes, but it grew spiritually and geographically also. Sadly, growth of the Christian church became less of a priority in the latter years of Christendom. Especially in the twentieth century, pluralism and laxity have taken their toll on the growth of the Christian faith in Europe and North America. At the same time, the church in Africa and Asia has grown remarkably!

Healthy congregations seek to be growing deep and wide. This means the congregation's life is structured around Jesus' Great Commission: "Go therefore and make disciples of all nations, baptizing them . . . and teaching them" (Matthew

28:19-20). God has chosen to use us as workers in the garden of life. Paul wrote, "I planted, Apollos watered, but God gave the growth. So neither the one who plants nor the one who waters is anything, but only God who gives the growth" (1 Corinthians 3:6-7). God, through human service, grows more and better disciples in every corner of the world.

Movement

The third characteristic of life is movement. Amoebas move through their environment, morning glories array themselves to catch the full light of the sun, and the church moves forward toward God's future destination of the last day. The healthy church is moving forward. It has caught a vision from God and is actively moving toward that vision into its future.

Movement generates energy and momentum. The healthy congregation is perpetually in prayer to discern Christ's direction for its future. This prayerful attitude opens the congregation to the Holy Spirit's leading and infectious and life-giving energy.

In the physical world momentum is measured by the equation: $F = ma$ (Force equals mass times acceleration). The size and strength of the congregation multiplied by its acceleration toward the kingdom's goals produces compelling force. Such momentum is an underrated factor in group dynamics, especially within the church. The congregation that knows where Christ wants it to go, and is actively pursuing that course, becomes an exciting attraction to the world. This spiritual momentum creates its own excitement within the body of Christ, inviting believers into the future for which we pray: "Thy kingdom come." Momentum is also inviting to unchurched people who want to experience God's transformative power in their lives. When they see God changing a congregation they are drawn to this same transformational momentum for their own lives.

The healthy congregation sees God at work in two dimensions simultaneously: God works with us both as individuals and as a gathered community. In each arena God's purpose is to move us from lament to praise, from sin to sanctification, from self toward God. Power for this movement lies within the Holy Spirit who "calls, gathers, enlightens, and sanctifies the whole Christian church on earth," as Martin Luther wrote in his explanation of the third article of the Apostles' Creed.[8] As individuals and as the gathered people of God, we are moving toward God's ultimate fulfillment of God's kingdom.

Transformation

All living organisms exhibit metabolism. The Greek word from which we derive our word *metabolism* means "to change." Healthy organisms metabolize; that is, they transform complex chemical and physical matter for use within the body. The metabolic process of healthy living organisms liberates the power needed to sustain life. Even though the metabolic process cannot readily be seen by the naked eye, it is still essential to life.

For the purpose of describing the healthy congregation we might use the synonym *transformation. Transformation* is a Greek word that means "to change across form." This is exactly what a plant does when it takes carbon dioxide and makes oxygen. Healthy congregations serve the gospel by being communities where faith transforms individual members. The apostle Paul had this in mind when he wrote to the Romans: "Do not be conformed to this world, but be transformed by the renewing of your minds, so that you may discern what is the will of God—what is good and acceptable and perfect" (Romans 12:2). This is faith transforming lives, reshaping them in the image of Christ. It is a process that has no quantitative or qualitative measure. It can only be inferred from the testimonies of individual believers as to the life change produced by the good news.

Sensitivity

Biologists use the curious term *irritability* to describe the next hallmark of life. In its classic biological definition, *irritability* is defined as an organism's sensitivity to stimulation in its immediate surroundings. Whether it is the coagulant reaction of the blood to a skin wound or the immune system's response to a foreign virus, living organisms have the ability to sense changes in themselves or in their surroundings. Stimuli may come from within or from without to challenge the body. These stimuli sometimes threaten to upset the body's healthy balance, thereby causing disease. Without the ability to sense these changes, living things would be constantly in peril.

Sensitivity is vital to the healthy congregation. It must be able to feel the stimuli that threaten to upset it. Rumor and gossip, conflict, and difficult people all pose significant challenges to the congregation. Whether or not the church can sense these challenges may drive the congregation into disease or may bring about new life.

Therefore, an essential feature of vital, energetic congregations is how they manage the inevitable conflict that comes with change and people living in community. It is a sign of healthy vitality for congregations to face their conflicts, both by calling them out into the open and by nurturing each other through rough waters.

Adaptation

Profound changes in an organism's environment require an adaptive response or the organism dies. Life adapts. Witness the example of the flounder, which changes its color and pattern to match its environment, or note the change in the wing pattern of an African butterfly to mimic other distasteful butterflies in an effort to avoid predators.

The healthy congregation as a living entity must also adapt to its context in order to retain its relevance. All the sensitivity in the world would be of little benefit to the body of Christ without the ability to adapt. While the truth of the gospel never changes, our world is radically changing at increasing speed, requiring the congregation to adapt to new methods and models. The challenges posed by contemporary culture never cease. How will the congregation adapt? Will it stick its collective head in the sand? Or will it trust God and each other enough to discuss the issues, pray for Christ's direction, and stretch forth into the world to be salt and light?

Reproduction

Living things reproduce themselves. "If there is any one characteristic that can be said to be the *sine qua non* [without which there would be nothing] of life, it is the ability to reproduce."[9] One of the most basic principles in biology is that living things come from other living things. It is no different in the life God gives through faith.

Ever since Jesus called twelve men to be disciples, the church has actively sought to reproduce Christian followers. Catechizing both youth and new believers and planting daughter churches and new mission starts are all reproductive functions characteristic of healthy congregations. This mind-set of seeking to reproduce faith draws the church outside of itself to serve the world. It is altogether too easy to view a congregation as a place to get one's personal needs met or to just take care of the present membership. This is an unhealthy attitude that will quickly bring an end to a church family's lineage: no children are brought to faith, no daughter churches are begun, no domestic or foreign missions are established. The inevitable result is death.

Life cycles

There is one more facet of biological life that is of interest to organizations like the church. All living things follow a predictable life-cycle pattern: birth, growth, adolescence, maturity, decline, and, finally, death. This pattern is illustrated by the normal curve or, as it is also known, the bell-shaped curve (see figure 1.1).

What this means for congregations, even for the healthiest congregations in our denominations, is that death is as inevitable as growth and maturity. This should not surprise the Christian church, which regularly walks alongside people from birth to the grave. The normal curve teaches us several important realities that, if taken to heart, will radically reshape congregational mission. The first is that churches will die. Just like our most gifted pastors and lay ministers who minister to the dying in hospice settings, nursing homes, and oncology centers,

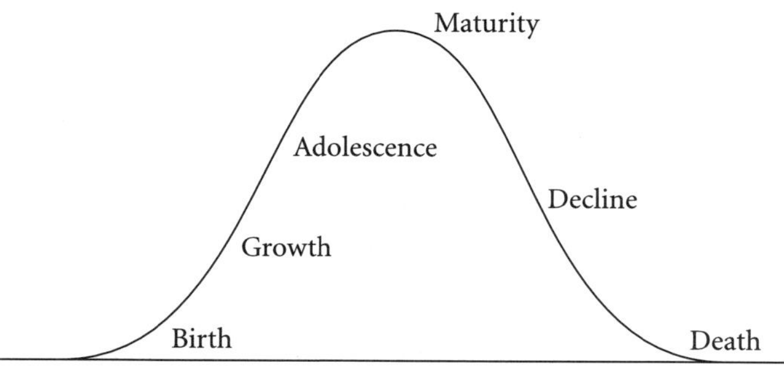

Fig. 1.1. Source: Patrick Lattore (unpublished lecture, Fuller Theological Seminary, Pasadena, Calif., July 1998).

gifted leaders can help congregations die gracefully. This is not a lack of faith on our part but rather a recognition of God's plan in creation. To praise God and close the doors might be the most faithful statement the congregation can make to its community. The death of a congregation is no more a threat to the Christian church than the death of an individual threatens the human race.

Looking at the normal curve with regard to congregations might also cause us to think in new paradigms about the life of the local congregation. In reality, there are many groupings of congregants within each particular congregation. Figure 1.2 illustrates a possible approach of giving birth to new "congregations" within the existing one. Youth ministry, small-group ministry, and worship settings in other languages might qualify as harmonic life cycles that will increase the life span of the congregation.

A much more difficult task is to create paradigm shifts while the church is still in the adolescent stage of growth, before maturity and decline thrust the congregation into the death spiral. The illustration in figure 1.3 depicts this artful shift to anticipate the next generation of new ideas, methods, and ministries. Anticipating the future well beforehand is a difficult process for all organizations.

It was Job who long ago reminded us all to "ask the animals, and they will teach you; the birds of the air, and they will

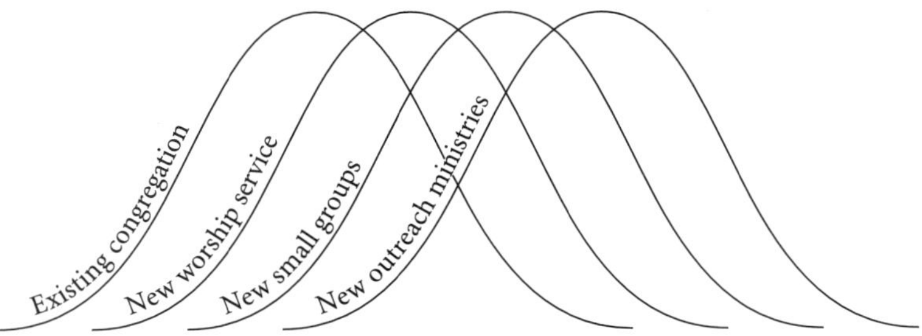

Fig. 1.2. Source: Patrick Lattore (unpublished lecture, Fuller Theological Seminary, Pasadena, Calif., July 1998).

tell you; ask the plants of the earth, and they will teach you; and the fish of the sea will declare to you. Who among all these does not know that the hand of the LORD has done this? In his hand is the life of every living thing and the breath of every human being" (Job 12:7-10). We can indeed learn God's consistent design of healthy life by observing the created world. Applying what we glean from that observation will serve us in building healthy congregations.

Turning toward health

Now that we have a grasp on what a healthy congregation looks like, we focus our attention on the task of turning around a plateaued or declining congregation. An unhealthy congregation in need of a turn around is recognizable by its deficiency in one or more of the previously mentioned criteria. The thesis of this book is that, while some congregations ought to be allowed to die gracefully, many others can address their systemic ill health and once again become the dynamic, vibrant body that Christ desires. Such a turn around toward health will require both pastoral and lay leaders who are able to walk a membership through a process of discerning Christ's vision for mission in its unique setting.

Toward this end, chapter two begins with analyzing the problem of declining churches in the United States and Canada.

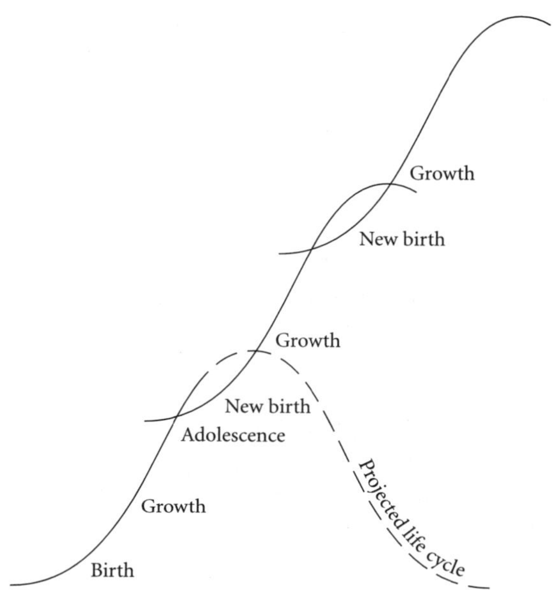

Fig. 1.3. Source: Patrick Lattore (unpublished lecture, Fuller Theological Seminary, Pasadena, Calif., July 1998).

Applying the holistic definition of church health to actual congregational life sheds light on the reality of congregational decline. With this foundation we then begin to specifically address the congregation's turn around in five phases: design, study, plan, act, and tend. These stages are built upon the insightful work of Kennon L. Callahan and Ian B. Tanner in *Twelve Keys to an Effective Church: The Study Guide.* [10]

Chapter three introduces the *design* phase. In this phase leaders seek to create a process that can move the entire congregation from its present state toward its hoped-for future. To achieve this future, in the *study* phase leaders and the congregation work to clearly distinguish the church's mission from its vision. Clarifying these separate but related concepts is the goal of chapter four. In the study phase the congregation also needs to honestly assess its current health and the attendant reasons for its decline and ill health. Chapter five outlines how the congregation can work toward this necessary self-awareness.

Next we move on to the *plan* phase. Vision and leadership are the essential ingredients in all congregational turn arounds. Chapter six outlines the tools to kindle a vision that is created and owned by the congregation. The goal of chapter seven is to strengthen the congregation's leadership for the turn around.

With this accomplished, the congregation moves to the *act* phase. Inevitably, there will be obstacles to overcome once the congregation has agreed upon a new vision for its future and developed its leadership skills to enable that new vision. Concrete steps to hurdle these obstacles is the subject of chapter eight. Chapter nine offers proven mission strategies for the congregation to consider for action.

The fourth and final phase is to *tend* this newfound vision for mission. Vigilantly tending the vision, implementing it and refining it, will stretch for years to come. Chapter ten discusses how to continually refresh and refine the vision, evaluate the mission strategies implemented, and gather new information as circumstances change.

With God's grace, health and vitality can be reclaimed and churches can indeed be turned around!

Reflection questions

1. Recall Christ Church as described on the opening pages of this chapter. Do worship visitors get the sense that your congregation is vibrant and healthy like Christ Church?

2. Where do you see God's gift of life breathed into the body of Christ, which is your congregation?

3. How might the seven criteria of life—organization, growth, movement, transformation, sensitivity, adaptation, and reproduction—be used to describe the health of your congregation?

Notes

1. Claude A. Villee, Warren F. Walker Jr., and Robert D. Barnes, *General Zoology*, 5th ed. (Philadelphia: W. B. Saunders Co., 1978), 15–18.

2. Peter Steinke, *Healthy Congregations: A Systems Approach* (Bethesda, Md.: Alban Institute, 1996), vii.

3. Donald A. McGavran, *The Bridges of God* (New York City: Friendship Press, 1955).

4. Keith Green, "Asleep In The Light." Copyright © 1978 Birdwing Music/Ears To Hear Music/Cherry Lane Music Publishing, Co. Inc.

5. Elmer Towns, as quoted in "Reflecting on the Church Growth Movement," *Ministry Advantage* 7, no. 4 (fall 1997): 8.

6. Rick Warren, *The Purpose Driven Church: Growth Without Compromising Your Message & Mission* (Grand Rapids, Mich.: Zondervan Publishing House, 1995), 17.

7. Christian A. Schwarz, *Natural Church Development: A Guide to Eight Essential Qualities of Healthy Churches* (Carol Stream, Ill.: ChurchSmart Resources, 1996), 7.

8. Martin Luther, *The Small Catechism by Martin Luther in Contemporary English with Lutheran Book of Worship Texts (1979 Edition)* (Minneapolis: Augsburg Publishing House; Philadelphia: Fortress Press, 1979), 14–15.

9. Villee, Walker, Barnes, *General Zoology*, 17.

10. Kennon L. Callahan and Ian B. Tanner, *Twelve Keys to an Effective Church: The Study Guide* (San Francisco: HarperSanFrancisco, 1992), 7.

2 Hallmarks of Congregational Health
Recognizing Congregational Decline

This sickness doth infect
The very life-blood of our enterprise.

1 Henry IV 4.1.28-29

Gloria Dei Church, formed in 1953, is just a five-minute drive from the heart of its state's capital city. The congregation bought an excellent piece of property located in the midst of a vital neighborhood filled with large middle-income families transplanted from the Midwest. The founding pastor of the congregation was morally conservative and possessed a gift for liturgical worship and a strong belief in the ministry of the laity. From its founding, the congregation had a vision to be a racially mixed congregation. Occupying nearly nine acres, almost unfathomable in size for its time, the congregation also had a vision to begin a school for gifted children, a need the congregation believed was not being met in the community.

In the years since Gloria Dei's founding, urban sprawl and the graying of the population have changed the surrounding community dramatically. Over the past forty years, the makeup of the neighborhood has changed because of an influx of immigrants. Many of the neighborhood's original families have moved to the outskirts of the city twenty-five minutes away.

Eight hundred people worshiped at Gloria Dei at its peak in 1964. Eight years later a congregational split reduced the congregation's average attendance to four hundred. Sadly, the trend continued to spiral downward so that by 1988 attendance was two hundred, and in 1993 it had fallen to its lowest point at ninety-eight people present for worship. This tragic decline was the result of multiple factors: conflict in the congregation over the school and between the pastor and the school principal. Turmoil also erupted within the congregation over the denomination's stand on homosexuality. The congregation lost trust with the senior pastor over how he communicated with the membership about these issues.

It would be easy to diagnose Gloria Dei's problem solely in terms of membership decline. In fact, this is how most congregations in this predicament see their situation. How can we get more members who will give more money? Growth alone does not make for congregational health, as discussed in the previous chapter. If the fantasy of the membership were fulfilled overnight and four hundred more people sat in the pews each Sunday, each one making substantial contributions, the congregation would still be unhealthy.

More than membership decline

The problems of Gloria Dei must be seen in a broader context if it is to be turned around to health. While lack of growth is the most obvious and immediate threat to survival, in the long-term lack of organization and no forward movement are equally damaging. Energy expended that does not result in people's lives being transformed by the gospel is fruitless and also a threat to survival. Insensitivity to the needs of unchurched neighbors along with inadequate adaptation to context and culture or an absence of reproduction of faith will just as predictably lead to congregational death.

Deeper analysis of the congregation's story reveals these hidden threats and offers insight for a treatment plan for this unhealthy body of Christ. The congregation suffered while the members became closed in on themselves and lost trust with their denomination over a single issue. Growth diminished as a result. Resting on its laurels after creating and building a wonderful parochial school, the congregation lost momentum toward a new goal in service to the kingdom. Vitality of faith decreased as activities in the congregation centered less around prayer, Bible study, and ministry. Members were losing commitment while the gospel was not transforming their lives. Decline was inevitable; death was imminent.

Centuries ago, Sir Isaac Newton discovered one of the fundamental principles of the physical universe, which we might paraphrase as: "A body at rest tends to stay at rest unless acted upon by another force." As a physicist rather than a church leader, Newton could not possibly have realized that this physical law is also applicable to the body of Christ. By observing falling ecclesiastical bodies we can correctly deduce that congregations at rest tend to stay at rest unless acted upon by an outside force.

Gloria Dei is a classic illustration of this principle. Sadly, it is not alone. The trends for the Christian church in the United States and Canada are sobering. Milton Coalter, John Mulder, and Louis Weeks draw a clear picture in their 1996 book, *Vital Signs: The Promise of Mainstream Protestantism.*[1] They cite statistics from 1965 to 1990 indicating alarming membership decline in such mainline Protestant churches as the American Baptist Church (down 1.5 percent), the United Methodist Church (down 19.5 percent), and the Episcopal Church USA (down 57.8 percent).[2] This phenomenon of decline is made all the worse when one factors in the increase in the general population of the United States in that same time frame. In 1965 the United States held 194,303,000 people while in 1990 the population soared to 248,709,873, a 28 percent increase in population.[3]

Unofficial estimates in the Evangelical Lutheran Church in America suggest that as many as one-third of its nearly eleven thousand existing congregations are in danger of not surviving the next ten to fifteen years! Looking at congregations like Gloria Dei, it would be too easy to blame changing neighborhoods as the reason for this widespread decline. The problem is much bigger than that simple diagnosis. A 1994 study by the ELCA Department for Research and Evaluation titled *A Profile: Facts about the Congregations of the Evangelical Lutheran Church in America,*[4] found that fully 39 percent of ELCA congregations were declining in a growing community! Far too many

Christian congregations in the United States have fallen into poor overall health and are dying regardless of their location or demographics.

Focusing the issue

To clarify the dilemma of declining churches we first need to separate the issues. Much of the current discussion on how to turn around congregations becomes muddied for lack of a distinction between the needs and problems of existing congregations versus new mission starts or congregational restarts. A mission start is a congregation that is intentionally planted by a denomination or by a mother congregation. A restart is a congregation that once had a viable ministry but has declined to the point of death and has had to be restarted again almost as if it were a new mission start.

Wabash Church was a country church for many years until the suburbs of the nearby metropolis began to close in. It still sits beyond the outer ring of suburbs in the middle of dairy farms, well away from major arterial roads. Membership dwindled to an average of twenty or fewer worshipers a Sunday. This congregation was essentially restarted as if it were a new mission plant.

The remarkable restart of Wabash Church broke all the rules. It had an exceptionally poor location in a farming area far from traffic patterns. It had little in the way of building and even less staffing. A new vision, with lay and pastoral leadership focused on that common vision, generated forward movement resulting in the congregation's rapid growth to nearly eight hundred in worship attendance each Sunday. As it grew, Wabash addressed its ill health and is now one of the healthiest churches in its community.

Restarts, like mission congregation plants, have a luxury not afforded to existing congregations. The common denominator between restarts and mission plants is the relative ease of achieving a clearly articulated, universally owned vision. The entrepreneurial leaders of the new mission start share a common vision of what the Holy Spirit is leading them toward. Likewise, the members of a congregation at death's door painfully understand their crisis. Through prayer and fervent faith they arrive at a renewed vision, again universally or very nearly universally shared, that reinvigorates the body with new life. Restarts and new missions, by virtue of having so few members, have a greater opportunity to address the obstacles they face in creating a healthy place for spiritual growth.

Established congregations, those more than thirty-five years old, often find themselves in the mature to declining stages of their organizational life cycles. These established congregations have more difficulties than restarts or mission plants. While they may still maintain viable worship attendance, giving, and congregational programs, as well as adequate buildings and property, they also have traditions, history, and hidden conflicts to overcome among a greater number of people. It is far more complicated to build a common vision among 250 people with a long history together than among a remnant of twenty, as in the case of Wabash, or to begin with two as in the story of Saddleback Valley Community Church in Mission Viejo, California.

Currently, there are any number of well-known congregational models to which church leaders flock for insight that might stem decline. Congregations like Willow Creek Community Church, South Barrington, Illinois (a mission start); Saddleback Valley Community Church (mission start); Community Church of Joy, Glendale, Arizona (a restart); and Overlake Christian Church, Redmond, Washington (a restart) perhaps are not the best models for existing congregations that have fallen into ill health. The issues faced by these star congregations to reach their present state of vitality differ greatly from older, established churches seeking to turn around. There is no single, magic program that can be translated from these stellar congregations to painlessly turn around a plateaued congregation.

What can pastors and lay leaders do to correct this dire situation of plateaued or declining congregations within a growing population? How can members who deeply love Christ and care for their congregation turn around their particular body of Christ into a healthy place once again? Mike Regele, founder of Percept Group, a company that supplies demographic information to churches and denominations, puts the matter simply but forcefully: "The Church has a choice: to die as a result of its resistance to change or to die in order to live."[5]

For the church willing to die and rise again, the place to begin is to search out new models based on congregations that have successfully turned around. Examining such congregations will provide answers to this cross-denominational problem. One source of assistance can be found in the research of George Barna. Barna is a pollster who has significantly advanced our understanding of models for turn-around churches. No analysis of this phenomenon would be complete without reference to Barna's important work on the subject, titled *Turnaround Churches*.[6]

Barna took a "snowball sampling" of thirty churches in sixteen states. A snowball sample, while not a classical quantitative research method, is a study that takes a small, but representative, sampling and seeks to draw conclusions valid for the larger group. His study included congregations that had once been vital, healthy communities but had experienced a rapid downturn, and then later turned around their stagnation, returning to health once again. The congregation and pastors underwent extensive interviews designed to extract the most important elements in their renewal.

Barna's research bears sobering news for plateaued or declining congregations. He asserts: "When a church takes a nosedive in attendance or membership, it generally does not make a comeback. The typical experience seems to be that, once a church loses its momentum, the most probable outcome is either death or stabilization at a much smaller size."[7]

Gleaned from his research sample, eight symptoms of decline have been identified by Barna. *Demographic changes* in the surrounding community are an obvious symptom. So too is *inadequate leadership* that fails to lead, motivate, or channel the congregation's ministry. *Poor management* cripples the ministry from accomplishing what it sets out to do. Not surprising,

Barna lists *old blood* as the fourth common symptom of decline. By "old blood" Barna means that the congregation has few young adults and children and the same people end up doing all the work year in and year out. *Building campaigns* expose and create conflict and are the fifth symptom of downward spirals. A sixth symptom is found in a congregation that has become an *ingrown family* that focuses on caring for itself instead of serving others in mission. *Resistance to change* is a seventh major factor in congregational decline. Finally, a congregation in *poor spiritual health* quickly devolves into becoming a social club with a cross. Members look busy and active but have lost their zeal for mission.

Surveying this landscape of congregational ill health in the United States and Canada is not for the faint of heart. Faced with the startling statistics and these painful symptoms, the reality of turning around a declining congregation is daunting indeed. "The bad news," Barna writes, "is that the odds of experiencing such a turn around are slim."[8] Such slim results are found not only in congregations near death's door, but in any congregation that has experienced a sustained downward trend. In spite of this seeming pessimism, we must remember that we serve a God who is in the business of death and resurrection. Without doubt, Regele is right: the church must die to itself and its old patterns and allow God to resurrect it anew.

Examining models like the ones Barna lifts up can be extremely useful. Finding other models in the same geographic area or in congregations similar in ministry context can be even more helpful. Yet, turning around a congregation with such major problems requires a more thorough diagnosis in order to select the proper treatment.

Signs of ill health

Diagnosing the severity of the problem with simplistic answers to these complex dysfunctions will actually make matters worse rather than better. Therefore, let us return to our sevenfold definition of a healthy congregation and examine what an unhealthy congregation would look like in each of these broad categories.

Poor organization

It is not difficult to imagine the multitude of problems poor organization creates in a congregation. Organizational problems run the full spectrum: from wasting precious human resources in too many meetings to producing leaders who protect their own budgets and programs instead of working for the congregation's common vision. Or as we learned from George Barna, inadequate leadership and poor management contribute to poor organizations. Inescapably, decline results from leaders who will not lead anywhere, just as it results from leaders who cannot manage the details needed to get there. Organizational problems breed low morale, discouragement, and failure. These trends inevitably lead downward.

The apostle Paul's references to the gifts of the Holy Spirit remind us that administration and leadership are gifts from God (Romans 12:4-8; 1 Corinthians 12:4-11,28; Ephesians 4:7-13). There is no congregation that does not have present within its membership people with either of these gifts. These people possess the God-given talent necessary to effectively lead and organize the congregation's ministry. The question is, Who will get out of the way to let them use their gifts to the glory of God?

No growth

Christ Church welcomes an average of one hundred new members each year. These new persons add fresh perspective, energy, and momentum to the congregation. The twist to Christ Church's story is that it serves a nearby Army post and an Air Force base; most of these new members are recently transferred military personnel and their families. So, there is also an annual loss of about one hundred members because of transfers to new posts or bases around the world. For twenty years the net change in the congregation's membership numbers has been zero, but this dynamic congregation still meets the health criteria of growth. Because of its health in the other aspects, Christ Church is attractive to new persons in the community. This growth, although balanced by reduction, promotes continued health.

Congregations that experience no growth or precious little growth suffer from a lack of evangelism. Evangelism refers to sharing the gospel and often is seen as a bold, outward expression of dynamic faith. A deficiency in evangelism can result from several factors. Lack of evangelism may be due to poor faith transformation through the preaching and teaching ministries of the congregation, resulting in an insecure faith among members. Or it may stem from inadequate faith transformation that produces a shallow faith with no zeal to share the good news with others. Or perhaps members, sensing their church is not moving forward, are not enthusiastic about their congregation and simply do not invite outsiders. Maybe it is because the congregation has a history of burying its conflict and frightening members away from bringing their friends and neighbors. Whatever the reason, it is necessary to dig out the root cause and treat it, rather than put a bandage over the symptoms.

No forward movement

The congregation with no clear sense of forward direction is a congregation that has lost its sense of purpose. What is it about? Why does it exist? What distinguishes the congregation from local service clubs? In addition, the congregation with no forward movement does not know itself very well. What are the congregation's strengths? What does it do better than the other local congregations? Not to mention that a congregation with no forward movement has failed to grasp community needs that it has the God-given resources to address. Putting purpose, self-assessment, and community needs together will powerfully drive the congregation forward.

A more severe cause of lack of forward movement is a deficiency of faith. The story of Scripture is the story of God working with individuals and the corporate group at the same time. When there is no forward movement by the congregation, faith within this larger set is, at least, underdeveloped. At worst, faith is absent. To move into an uncertain and frightening future is a supreme act of faith on the part of any group. This is precisely the witness of the congregation that professes to be Christian. The unchurched world is eager to find such faith in a culture filled with uncertainty and despair. Struggling together to find God's will is a difficult but exceptionally rewarding facet of life in the Christian congregation.

Ineffective transformation of faith

Ananias and Sapphira in Acts 5:1-11 serve as excellent examples of individuals in whom the gospel was unable to take root and grow. This couple thought they could fool the church. Like Jesus' parable of the seed that fell on the rocky ground (Matthew 13:1-9; Mark 4:1-9; Luke 8:4-8), the good news did not have soil enough to grow unto harvest. Congregations that behave as Ananias and Sapphira did lose over time their centeredness in Jesus Christ and become outposts of social activism or turn into community service clubs instead of Christian churches. Barna's research is accurate: poor spiritual health—that is, ineffective faith transformation—is indeed a profound symptom of ill health.

No pastor or lay leader can directly assure that the gospel is being integrated fully into the individual lives of the congregation. This is a matter of the Holy Spirit speaking in that still, small voice inside the hearts of women and men. It is, however, within the realm of pastors and lay leaders to work diligently to see that the gospel is proclaimed through preaching and teaching and that the sacraments are administered faithfully. Leadership is responsible for focusing the congregation's energies on the Christian basics of worship, prayer, witness, and service.

Insensitivity

One of the most common causes of congregational ill health is conflict that is not addressed. Conflict is especially deadly to the church because of the widespread myth that conflict should not exist amid the Christian church. As we shall examine further in chapter nine, conflict is to be expected wherever there are people. Burying the conflict beneath polite Christian smiles is rather like putting a bandage over a skin boil, hoping that the infection will just disappear. Instead, it will infect the rest of the body!

In reality, hidden conflict is an indicator of the insensitivity of the congregation. The congregation has shut off its sensitivity to its own pain. Callousness in turn prevents the group from dealing with its disagreements. An illustration of this can be found in Barna's research where he lists building campaigns as a symptom of decline. Building programs in themselves do not cause congregational ill health. It is the hidden dysfunction in the membership brought out by the campaigns that causes disease. The inability to sense these submerged dynamics prior to the building campaign is the real culprit.

Barna also lists resistance to change as an indication of decline. This too is a result of insensitivity to the context and culture of the congregation. The membership has closed off its senses, thus limiting its ability to react to change. The irony is that the congregation believes it is preserving its integrity by resisting change when it is truly committing suicide.

Insufficient adaptation

Ever since the Council of Jerusalem between Peter and Paul was held over the issue of whether Christians should continue to practice Jewish laws, the church has needed to adapt to changing contexts and cultures. Perhaps, given the speed of change in our age, this is even more true today. The different generations present in today's congregations each have their own capacity to deal with the speed of change. Our youngest generations have grown up in a world where computers become obsolete within six months, in contrast to the older generations that matured when change came much more slowly.

Barna lists changes in community demographics as a symptom of decline. The truth is, although the neighborhood is different from when the congregation was formed, there are still unchurched people surrounding the church property! Study after study arrives at the same conclusion: the percentage of people in the United States and Canada who are churched is decreasing in proportion to the growing population. Congregations that adapt to these changes can continue vital ministry no less than when they were planted.

Another manifestation of the need to adapt can be found in the current crisis in our churches over style of music. Congregations that have failed to accommodate themselves to their unique ministry setting in terms of music tastes are faltering and declining. Most likely, members are also fighting each other over this issue as well. The inability to adapt leads to dysfunction and, ultimately, death.

Lack of reproduction

Why is the Dead Sea dead? Because, as this old preaching illustration points out, the Dead Sea has no outlet. A congregational system that does not actively reproduce itself becomes just as closed and dead as the Dead Sea. Christian congregations exist for the purpose of sharing the gospel with the world. Their function is to deliver a message that, through the work of the Holy Spirit, results in reproduction. Failure to communicate the good news to our children so the Spirit can transform their lives into living, active faith is a failure to reproduce.

Barna's snowball sample uncovered old blood as a characteristic of declining congregations. This is a problem of not reproducing faith and leadership in succeeding generations. Without new leaders with the faith to carry on the congregation's ministry, there is no future for the body.

Each of these measures of health exhibits complex interactions with one another. It is difficult to sort out just one to the exclusion of the others. They are mutually dependent. Congregational health is a delicate and broad-based balance of all seven of these variables.

A turn around

For the purposes of this book the term "turn-around congregation" is used to describe a congregation that has reversed an unhealthy trend of more than five years in one or more of these seven health factors. As you might imagine, this is a most arduous task. It will require many things but most especially a grounding in Word and Sacrament and prayer, courage, and faith on the part of pastor(s) and lay leaders. Why is it so hard to turn around a congregation? Nicolò Machiavelli gave one answer in his famous work, *The Prince*:

> And it ought to be remembered that there is nothing more difficult to take in hand, more perilous to conduct, or more uncertain in its success, than to take the lead in the introduction of a new order of things. Because the innovator has for enemies all those who have done well under the old conditions, and lukewarm defenders in those who may do well under the new. This coolness arises partly from fear of the opponents, who have the laws on their side, and partly from the incredulity of men, who do not readily believe in new things until they have had a long experience of them.[9]

Reformers within the congregation will be opposed by those who enjoyed the fruits of the previous season of ministry. And because few people live their own lives with any sense of personal vision, there will be a slow reluctance to move out of the old, painful patterns that have laid waste to the congregation.

The only outside force capable of rejuvenating congregations with such histories is the Holy Spirit. The authentic spiritual growth necessary for the renewal of troubled congregations comes only through God's Spirit working in mysterious ways. Certainly in the history of the church there have been instances of growth based solely on personality, fad, political correctness, or civil religion. But as the wise Rabbi Gamaliel argued before the Sanhedrin: "If this plan or this undertaking is of human origin, it will fail" (Acts 5:38).

Mysteriously, the Holy Spirit chooses to work in our world through human beings. God working through the Spirit uses our intellect, passion, and service to bring about God's kingdom. The force of the Holy Spirit moves through God's servants to accomplish a congregational turn around. It is not a task for the timid! Sir Isaac Newton also noted that with any force there is also an opposing force: friction. This applies to congregational circumstance, as well as to physical reality.

Gloria Dei's turn around

Pastor Chuck accepted the call to Gloria Dei in 1994. He did so fully aware that this was a congregation in need of a turn around. He understood the odds against success and he grasped the enormity of the task. Four years later, Gloria Dei, through exceptional hard work, courage, and profound faith, was able to turn its ministry around. Worship attendance has more than doubled from its low point of ninety-eight, and stewardship has increased likewise. Bible studies have sprung up and a contagiously exciting youth ministry is once more in place. Pastor Chuck also reaches out to the gang leaders in the neighborhood to tell them that God loves them. Gloria Dei Church is once again a dynamic, healthy congregation.

The remainder of this book is dedicated to helping your congregation turn from a congregation experiencing symptoms of decline toward a community on the road to health. In that spirit, we move in chapter three to begin the five-phased process of a turn around: design, study, plan, act, and tend.

Reflection questions

1. Is your congregation strong enough now to undertake an attempt at a turn around or should it be considered a restart and begun anew as if it were just planted in your community?

2. Which of Barna's symptoms of decline are evidenced in your congregation? What are the contributing factors?

3. Of the seven characteristics of congregational health, where do you think your congregation is weakest? Strongest?

Notes

1. Milton J. Coalter, John M. Mulder, and Louis B. Weeks, *Vital Signs: The Promise of Mainstream Protestantism* (Grand Rapids, Mich.: W.B. Eerdmans Publishing Co., 1996).

2. Ibid., 21–22.

3. Bureau of the Census, *Statistical Abstract of the United States 1991: The National Data Book* 111th ed., prepared by the Economics and Statistics Administration, U.S. Department of Commerce, Bureau of the Census (Washington, D.C., 1991), 7.

4. Gretchen Olson, *A Profile: Facts About the Congregations of the Evangelical Lutheran Church in America* (Chicago: Department for Research and Evaluation, ELCA, 1994).

5. Mike Regele, *Death of the Church* (Grand Rapids, Mich.: Zondervan Publishing House, 1996), i.

6. George Barna, *Turnaround Churches: How to Overcome Barriers to Growth and Bring New Life to an Established Church* (Ventura, Calif: Regal Books, 1993).

7. Ibid., 17.

8. Ibid., 115.

9. Nicolò Machiavelli, *The Prince*, Encyclopaedia Brittanica's Great Books, 24th printing (Chicago: William Benton Publishers, 1982), 9.

3 Turning toward Health: Design
Designing the Turn-Around Process

First couple out to the couple on the right,
Form a star with the right hand cross.
Back with the left and don't get lost.
Swing your opposite with your right,
Now your partner with your left,
And on to the next.

Lloyd Shaw, *Cowboy Dances: A Collection of Western Square Dances*[1]

Imagine yourself western square dancing. Following the rhythm of the music, together with the instructions of the caller, you and your partner swirl and mingle, circle and promenade, change partners and change back, and finally return back "home."

The efforts at turning around a plateaued or declining congregation begin in much the same way. The dance of a turn around is a parade of partners: the pastor(s) and staff, the governing body, key opinion leaders, the general membership, in addition to the unseen partners—the larger community, including those the congregation hopes to reach with the gospel. Like a square dance, careful attention will be paid to the caller to be sure to follow where led. In this case, the caller is God who calls out the tune and keeps the music. Each member of the square is needed to dance his or her steps in harmony with one another for a revitalized congregation to replace the present dysfunctional or stagnant one.

The role of the pastor in this dance is critical. In a turnaround process, the pastor needs to give special attention to two things: prayer and leadership. The pastor sets the example for the congregation in prayer, seeking the will of God for the future of the congregation. In prayer, some of the dysfunction of the congregation begins to be addressed. Prayer leads the membership to give up its will and, through the power of prayer, replace it with God's will.

Leadership is the second hallmark of a pastor in a turn-around congregation. In this regard, it is imperative for the pastor to be one-half step ahead of the other dance partners. This is not to manipulate or force the process in any one direction. Rather, staying a half step ahead of the congregation enables the pastor to see the road ahead and anticipate what the process needs before it is needed. This prevents unnecessary delays and improves morale throughout the process. A nonanxious pastor who has faithfully prayed for God's guidance and who carefully leads into the future brings a calming presence to a membership beset by the unknown winds of change. This is of inestimable value to a turn-around congregation.

Moving around the square, we find the next set of partners. Congregation members in definable positions of leadership add their own step to the dance of revitalization. Their role is to initiate this entire endeavor. At the outset, they select the vision team and hand off the responsibility for designing the congregational process. Without their early stamp of approval, nothing from then on will succeed. Later, as the entire process unfolds, those people holding official leadership positions guide and shape the process, given their respective function in the congregational system. Any decisions that need to be made are brought by the vision team to these elected leaders to decide.

In the next corner of the square is the vision team. This team should be a group of lay leaders charged with design and oversight of the turn-around process. Like the pastor, they endeavor to remain one-half step ahead of the congregation as they build a process where the willing members of the congregation can decide their future together.

Those congregations with responsibilities to their larger denominational church bodies have other dance partners to whom they are accountable. Coordinating the steps of the congregation with the path of the denomination is essential to prevent collisions on the floor. And for all congregations, there are two silent dance partners involved in all this: the unchurched people to whom the congregation seeks to minister and the neighboring community. Involving these groups requires creativity and effort on the part of the congregation to discover their gifts and needs.

Shared vision

So just what will it take to turn around a congregation? The strongest method for accomplishing a turn around is to create a sweeping process that builds a congregationally based, God-given vision for mission. This is the dance. And like a dance, it cannot be done by the pastor alone, nor by the elected leadership independent from the pastor, or even by the membership. Neither can the turn around be accomplished by a small group sent off to devise a new vision for mission to be sold to the whole congregation.

Peter Senge, in his book *The Fifth Discipline: The Art and Practice of the Learning Organization*, offers an explanation for why such a method will never fully succeed. Senge states in his chapter "Shared Vision" that there are five possible outcomes when attempting a shared vision. These five possibilities are: commitment, enrollment, genuine compliance, formal compliance, and grudging compliance.[2] *Commitment* is the goal of all shared vision. It is when the members truly want the vision and will do what it takes to make it reality. *Enrollment*, he asserts, is one step below true commitment. Senge writes, "I can be thoroughly enrolled in your vision. I can genuinely want it to occur. Yet, it is still your vision."[3]

True commitment to the shared vision is rare. Only slightly more frequent is enrollment with the shared vision. The varying stages of *compliance*, on the other hand, are the most common reactions to a shared vision among a group. The genuinely compliant will understand the benefits of the vision and will do what is expected of them. Those in the formal compliance category do what the formal systems require of them but no more. The grudgingly compliant members do not buy into the group's vision for the future but will do what they have to do to maintain their positions of respect in the system.

The goal of this dance of turning around a plateaued or declining congregation is 100 percent genuine commitment. The reality is that will never happen. There will be proportionate representation at every point all along this scale. This makes the design of the process essential. The process needs to be structured to maximize the opportunities for members to become fully committed to the new vision. This is best achieved through their own involvement in the turn-around process. Congregational leadership that understands this scale of shared vision is better able to patiently move members up the scale from grudgingly compliant to higher stages.

To this end, a five-phased process—design, study, plan, act, and tend—is envisioned to get as many members to the commitment stage as possible. The lay out of this process enables the congregation to simultaneously address its health even as it positively focuses on the future Christ desires for it.

Design phase

The fivefold dance begins as the pastor and the elected leadership recognize the problems faced by the congregation. They need to design a process so that the maximum number of congregational members can determine the future. In creating this process, the first step is the selection of a vision team. The elected leadership of the congregation will appoint this team of competent leaders. The job of this ad hoc task force will be threefold: (1) Design a process by which the congregation decides on a vision for its future; (2) do the background research the congregation needs to build its vision; and (3) enhance communication within the congregation about the process.

How this vision team is structured is critical to achieve the best possible results. For this task force to succeed, it must be chaired by a respected and capable leader in the congregation. This needs to be a person of high skill who communicates well and can facilitate a group to accomplish a task. The chair also needs to be a person who is well respected by the entire membership and is seen as someone who is nonpartisan. Other desirable characteristics include vision, excellent listening skills, and the ability to concisely communicate the needs of others.

Choosing the membership of the task force also requires careful thought. Before selecting members for the vision team, elected leaders should first assess the natural constituencies in the congregation. A superior team is comprised of representatives of as many of the natural groups in the congregation as possible; for example, the choir, the fifty-somethings, the retirees, the young mothers, the dissident group, the old guard, the high school youth, the key opinion leaders, and so forth. From these constituencies, the elected leaders choose the key representatives to serve on the vision team. These members then naturally articulate the needs of their respective subgroup and relay back to that group the work of the task force. This builds trust in the system using the congregation's natural social architecture.

The pastor should be a member of this vision team as well. It is her or his calling from God to shepherd this flock toward the kingdom of God. This function cannot be abdicated nor delegated to another. The pastor, already one-half step ahead of the vision team, is looked to for biblical insight, expertise on the church, and visionary leadership. In this same manner, other key staff members might be considered to serve on this vision team alongside the pastor. However, the laity must make up the majority of the vision team in order to earn the greatest possible trust from the membership.

The size of the vision team depends upon the congregation. Too few on the team will mean poor representation of the general membership; too many will be unwieldy and make for an inferior team. It is better to attempt to build a vision team with six to twelve members with a strong representative mix and excellent personal gifts to bring to the team. Along the way, people with strengths not found on the vision team can be brought in from the congregation to accomplish varying tasks or to advise the vision team as needed. In this manner, more people take ownership of the process, excitement is generated in the congregation, and forward movement begins to accelerate into momentum.

Once constituted, the vision team must never go off by itself, work through all five phases alone, and return with a completed vision for the congregation's future. This will be perceived, and accurately so, as a "sales job." It will not matter how carefully crafted their work or how precise their assessment of the congregation. The best that can be hoped for in this scenario is genuine compliance, to use Senge's categories of shared vision. The congregation with an attitude of genuine compliance will never catch fire for the vision. It will never truly grab people and motivate them. Recall that the goal, rather, is that of commitment on the part of the membership. People are only committed to visions they have a hand in creating.

With the vision team in place and with its goals clearly before it, this ad hoc task force begins its work to design a process by which the congregation develops its vision for mission. This requires the vision team to spend time together planning and preparing long before calling the congregation into the turn-around enterprise. Just as with the pastor, the vision team needs to be one-half step ahead of the congregation throughout the five phases of the turn-around process.

The vision team is commissioned with designing the entire five-phased process. The first step is to design the remaining phases of study, plan, act, and tend. The team needs to lay out a road map for the entire work as best as it can see from its current perspective. A basic lay out of the next four phases creates a sense of security and reduced anxiety. At the same time the team must realize that greater clarity will be gained for the plan phase once the study phase is under way; likewise with the act and tend phases. The further along the process develops the more precise detail can be added to the overall turn-around endeavor.

Even given this limitation of foresight, a general lay out of all the pieces of the turn-around process is needed by the vision team. Think of it as choosing where to put the interstate highways on a map of the United States versus deciding long in advance where the stop signs will be. Later chapters of this book provide greater detail to the study, plan, act, and tend phases. Here is where the vision team needs to be slightly ahead of the congregation. Clarity among the vision-team members will reduce anxiety in the congregation.

Design goals

Three goals are critical to the vision team's design of the process: building common language and concepts, strengthening the faith of members, and creating a healthier life for the congregation.

Building common language and concepts

In designing the remaining process, the vision team must bear in mind that the study phase is where the work of the turn around begins for the membership. In the design the team seeks to develop a study phase that lays a foundation composed of common concepts and language for the membership to use to talk together about its problems and its future. The underlying assumption is that adults learn best when they discover new ideas for themselves rather than being told by an expert or even a trusted friend. The desired outcome of the entire turn-around process is for each member to have a moment of divine insight that breaks into his or her frozen pattern of thought and releases a new, shared vision for the congregation.

Strengthening faith

Along the way, as the team sets the foundation for the creation of a shared vision, another major mission goal will be achieved: the faith of each member will be strengthened. Vision is born in the personal encounter with the living God. When members wrestle with God, seeking a vision for the collective whole, they will find their own faith growing. In designing the next four phases, the vision team actively strives to connect members with God in a deeper level of communal trust and faith. This corporate experience of putting greater faith in God will then translate into the personal life of the member. This is the mystery of God's simultaneous corporate and individual shaping of the people of God.

Creating a healthier life together

A third goal of the design is to teach the congregation a new way of living together. Reasoning with each other from Scripture and praying together over tough issues will begin to engender trust within the membership that, especially in the troubled church, was not present before. Further, by members talking directly to other members, sociological and other barriers that have separated members from each other will begin to be bridged. Overcoming obstacles such as these is discussed in more detail in chapter nine.

Keys to a successful design

To increase the likelihood of a successful process and outcome, the following factors deserve consideration as part of the process design.

A diversity of members

The final design of the next four phases of the turn-around process calls for the best wisdom and creativity from the vision team. The team should make its goal to include all willing members of the congregation in the process, no matter how antagonistic they have been in the past. Children to senior citizens, all can have significant contributions as they bring their spiritual gifts to the mix. It is only when the body of Christ works as a unified whole that Christ's promise and vision is poured out to the church, sweeping it up in mission.

Calling forth these gifts in the body is of enormous aid to the vision team. One such resource the vision team might call is a member who is a teacher. Teachers understand the variety of learning styles people possess. A teacher can help the team devise a strategy whereby members with different learning styles can take in new information and process their experiences.

The reality is that processing new information takes time. Thus, the turn-around process cannot be rushed. It cannot be accomplished in an afternoon or even four afternoons, one for each of the next phases of study, plan, act, and tend. Adult learners need time to accommodate new ideas and assimilate them into their own world views. Racing through the process like a sprinter for the finish line will defeat the larger objectives.

Thorough and accessible research

The second stated goal of the vision team is to assemble the background research that the congregation needs to build its vision. The congregation needs to uncover its unique dysfunctions, assess its strengths, catalogue its current mission, and gain new learning about its surrounding community. The vision team needs to creatively organize itself to accomplish these objectives through a variety of methods. Assembling this information once it is gathered, however, is only a part of the task. With this newfound information, the harder task is to devise a means of enabling the congregation to draw its own conclusions from this data.

What shall the vision team research? Lovett Weems in his book *Church Leadership: Vision, Team, Culture, and Integrity* offers a substantial list.[4] Weems suggests gathering internal data on the congregation such as statistics on membership, attendance, and Sunday school, along with the age makeup of membership, actual giving, budget growth, and so forth. External data he suggests gathering include: local population, racial and ethnic mix, age and economic demographics, and traffic pattern statistics. Studying other congregations that have turned around and reading books on the subject are also part of the research task (see the bibliography at the end of the book). Only when the team members dive into the research will they begin to see a bigger picture of the data the congregation will need to best discern Christ's will.

Burying the congregation in facts and figures is less than helpful. Rather, the vision team needs to use its best judgment to determine just what the congregation needs to shape its future. How that material is presented is another critical factor. Displaying in a prominent place simple but well-done charts and graphs that can be quickly and easily understood can be helpful. Weeks in advance of a congregational vote, mailing to all members voter's guides that use the ballot language ensures there are no surprises.

Varying levels of involvement

Another factor that slows down the turn-around process is that members are willing to participate in a congregation's life at different levels. Some are only willing to attend worship while others are present whenever the church announces an activity. The committed core is the most likely group of participants to be actively involved in the process. A successful design seeks to include more than these dependable members, however. Involving worship participants generates more enthusiasm and ownership from a larger circle than the committed core.

And then there are some who attend only at Christmas and Easter. Designing the process for these varying levels of participation prepares for a broader shared vision. Strategies such as mailings and home visitations to discuss the mission and vision of the church with those members with the lowest involvement draws them into the shared vision. By the grace of God it may also activate some members whose participation has been low in the past.

Careful timing

The vision team also needs to account for the seasons of the year. It would be poor timing to begin the study phase just as the "snow birds" are all leaving for points south or just as school is letting out. Working around these seasonal constraints will slow down the process. This is to the congregation's advantage. Slowing down incites greater trust in the process and allows more time to analyze the present and consider the future.

Internal communication

From the beginning the vision team actively searches for ways to communicate with the congregation at every step of the process. Temple talks during worship, newsletter articles, first-class mailings, open forums, meeting minutes widely distributed, and committee sessions that are open to the membership are all necessary communication tools that must be used by the vision team. Consistent use of such multiple avenues of communication heads off mistrust, rumor, and other potential sources of conflict within the membership.

Lyle Schaller in his book *Strategies for Change* offers the principle of "redundant communication."[5] This involves the continual repetition of information to the congregation about what is happening as well as what has happened. Scripture too follows this pattern of reinforcement as seen in repetition of the covenant to Abraham or the mighty acts of God (consider Psalm 136 and others like it). The vision team should take every opportunity to remind the congregation of all the meetings that are and were open to it, all the public forums, announcements in worship, bulletin articles, mass mailings, and so forth. Schaller is correct when he notes that redundant communication is "one of the most effective means of minimizing unnecessary opposition."[6] No one can say they did not have a chance to be heard or participate. And it heads off people's spontaneous creation of information according to their perceived beliefs. (Addressing such rumors is explored in chapter nine).

Town hall forums are an efficient and effective method for the congregation to study itself. The vision team could host a number of such forums in which the congregation is broken into small groups for Bible study, discussion of information and problems, then, subsequently, for prayer. Members should be encouraged to participate in these small groups (round tables are perfect settings for these discussions) with members with whom they do not normally spend time. In so doing, members come face to face with other faithful believers who hold opinions and beliefs distinct from their own. Members will struggle with each other in these small units and then each group should report to the whole. This starts to shape commonality among the membership as themes begin to emerge from the gathering. An excellent facilitator from the congregation is needed to collect each group's report and summarize its contributions. These reports can be printed in the next Sunday's bulletin so that even those unwilling or unable to attend the forum are included. All the peripheral ideas shared can be gathered and disseminated to the existing ministries as "just go and do" items or saved for future ministry.

The next phase: study

With the design fleshed out the vision team turns to the study phase. This next phase seeks to address the truth about the congregation as well as introduce new information. Chapter four is designed to help the vision team and, subsequently, the congregation, clarify the vital distinction between mission and vision. Chapter five aids the vision team in the final shaping of the study phase so the congregation can assess its present circumstances and dysfunction.

"Do-si-do and mosey on home." The turn-around process has begun as all the partners form the square and dance to the music as the Heavenly Caller opens the future.

Reflection questions

1. What are the natural constituencies in your congregation? Who are the key opinion leaders in each of these groupings?

2. What other goals, specific to your congregation, should be used to guide the design of the turn-around process?

3. What will be the key to success in your unique context?

Notes

1. Lloyd Shaw, *Cowboy Dances: A Collection of Western Square Dances* (Caldwell, Idaho: Caxton Printers, Ltd., 1949), 63. Copyright © Lloyd Shaw Foundation. Used by permission.

2. Peter Senge, *The Fifth Discipline: The Art and Practice of the Learning Organization* (New York: Currency Doubleday, 1990), 219.

3. Ibid., 218.

4. Lovett H. Weems Jr., *Church Leadership: Vision, Team, Culture, and Integrity* (Nashville: Abingdon Press, 1993), 49–50.

5. Lyle Schaller, *Strategies for Change* (Nashville: Abingdon Press, 1993), 105.

6. Ibid.

4 Turning toward Health: Study
Distinguishing Mission and Vision

Go therefore and make disciples of all nations, baptizing them in the name of the Father and of the Son and of the Holy Spirit, and teaching them to obey everything that I have commanded you. And remember, I am with you always, to the end of the age.

Jesus
Matthew 28:19-20

At the outset of the study phase of a congregation's turn around, it is critical for willing members to wrestle with questions of mission and vision. First the pastor(s) and staff, then the vision team, and finally the congregation will benefit from in-depth Bible study and prayer over the mission of the congregation. In addition, the study phase begins with prayer that Christ may reveal to the body his unique vision for the congregation at this moment in history, given its surroundings as well as its gifts and abilities.

This is a crucial beginning because healthy congregations know their mission and have a clear vision of their future. Though *mission* and *vision* are often-used words in the church, these two words are in danger of becoming unusable because people define the terms so differently.

Nevertheless, mission and vision are indispensable concepts for the life of the church. This is especially so for the congregation for which these concepts have become so out of focus that the result has been congregational decline. Both the vision team and then the congregation need to rejuvenate these words in order to reform their ministry. The first task of the study phase is to define and distinguish these vital terms.

Mission

Pentecost was the beginning of the church of Jesus Christ. It was at Pentecost that God breathed the Spirit into the church, giving it life (Acts 2). The church lives only by God's energy, force, and will. This is exactly as Jesus promised at his ascension (Luke 24:48-51). Pentecost's fulfillment of this promise caused the disciples to look back at the last instructions of Jesus, commonly referred to as the Great Commission (see Matthew 28:19-20 and Mark 16:15). There the church finds its reason for being.

In the Great Commission, Jesus spoke straight to the point and, in the language of a direct command, he gave the disciples their marching orders. Jesus' last words define the church's central purpose. Any discussion of mission must begin here. Here is where the church returns to be reminded of its purpose.

Despite this crystal clear directive from our Lord, the church has long been confused over the distinction between mission and its cousin, vision. What is mission? How is it distinct from vision? Just where does our vision come from and who receives it? These are vital questions to be answered by the church that seeks to turn around. Clarity here will set the plateaued congregation on a track toward renewed health.

Let us begin by defining mission. Mission is the ongoing redemptive activity of God, working through the church, to reconcile the world unto God (see Romans 5:1-11; 2 Corinthians 5:18-20; Colossians 1:20). Mission is universal and active. It is the coming kingdom of God that breaks into history and changes lives. Mission begins within the individual, forms Christian community, and ends on the last day with the final and complete reign of God forevermore.

The importance of Jesus' mission imperative of Matthew 28 has not been completely lost on congregations of believers. Believers gathered by God's holy word have used Jesus' last instructions to create mission statements. Most congregations have one. Articles of incorporation begin with the mission statement while others go one step further and boil it down to a masthead slogan and design a letterhead featuring it. This is a wonderful first step. Sadly, it is often where congregations end their mission strategy.

The malaise of the Christian church in the United States and Canada can be directly linked to the lack of specificity inherent in the nature of Christ's mission. To go and make disciples, baptizing and teaching them whatever Jesus commanded, is a very broad commission. This is why the majority of congregations could exchange their mission statement with any other congregation, regardless of geography or theological tradition, and it would make little difference to their daily life. All congregations will preach, teach, administer the sacraments, counsel people who are troubled, visit people who are sick or imprisoned, and so on. With only this broad mission in hand each congregation looks like its neighbor down the street without distinction.

Here is where mission's cousin, vision, is needed. Vision gives specificity to the mission of a unique congregation of believers set within a particular geographical and cultural context at a given time. To illustrate this best, recall Paul's image of the body of Christ. "For just as the body is one and has many members, and all members of the body, though many, are one body, so it is with Christ," Paul writes in 1 Corinthians 12:12. Mission is the purpose of the entire body of Christ and each part of the body, whether the eye or the ear, serves that central purpose. And yet, each part of the body, whether the hand or the foot, has a very specific service to contribute that is unique to that part of the body. Vision identifies that unique service.

Vision

Vision is a frequently discussed word these days. It is a term heard in many circles, from the business realm to political parties, from educators to church leaders. As leaders from different fields search for the key components to success, the need for a clear, concise vision turns up in every discussion.

Within the realm of religion, the word *vision* has long been a part of our vocabulary. In fact, vision has been at the very core of religious experience. Vision is a central form of divine revelation that transfigures human thought beyond itself, turning it toward ultimate reality.

The word *vision* in both the Hebrew and Greek languages, much like in English, is derived from the basic verb "to see." Linguistically and metaphorically, a vision is "to see ahead." It is to see what someone else sees or to see a future far distant.

In Scripture, visions are given in states of wakefulness and sleep. They can provide messages for the present or future. In all cases they are particular, given to a messenger to deliver to God's people. In this way, vision becomes a servant of mission. Vision cannot and should not surpass nor suppress mission but rather grants it particularity for the cultural contexts in which God's people find themselves.

God is, by nature, a visionary. God has a vision for creation from the first word in Genesis through the ending verses of Revelation. The Old Testament speaks of the "last day" while New Testament Christians refer to the second coming of Christ. In the Revelation to John, chapter 21 describes this future God has in mind: "Then I saw a new heaven and a new earth; for the first heaven and the first earth had passed away, and the sea was no more. . . . And the one who was seated on the throne said, 'See, I am making all things new'" (vv. 1,5). This is a partial revelation of God's projected future, the complete understanding of which remains a mystery to mortals.

And yet, quite surprising to us, our God loves to reveal God's purpose and will to us. To this end, God grants vision to each congregation in accord with the grand vision God holds for the completion of all history. The visions given to the prophets of the Old Testament and the disciples in the New all harmonize with God's final plan.

Therefore, vision is always just beyond reach. A superior congregational vision based in God's vision for history lies just beyond the horizon. Once they are completed, visions that are within reach result in failure for the congregation.

For example, witness the U.S. quest in the 1960s to put a man on the moon by the end of the decade. The vision was set forth by President John F. Kennedy and swept up not only the country but the world. All the resources, science, and technology of the nation were brought to bear on this compelling vision. In its time, it seemed like an immense quest but was accomplished only eight years later. Though it was an unparalleled achievement, when it was over NASA floundered for the next twenty years. Not until Kennedy's vision was replaced by a vision to build a permanent space station did NASA recover its sense of direction.

In that same time period the Reverend Martin Luther King Jr. offered the nation a far more compelling and lasting vision. "I have a dream," said King, "that one day this nation will rise up and live out the true meaning of its creed: 'We hold these truths to be self-evident: that all men are created equal.'" It was a dream that outlived King and still motivates us into the future. This dream of racial equality is one that lies beyond the horizon. We can see it and stretch forth toward it but there will always be further to go.

The phenomenon of a spent vision like NASA's is repeated in many congregations that make a new building project their vision. For a time, vast amounts of energy and resources are marshaled for the vision of seeing new bricks and mortar added. But on completion, once the celebration is over, the movement of the congregation plateaus for lack of direction. Hidden conflict surfaces in the absence of a purposeful bearing and years may pass without the hoped-for increase in mission, unless the congregation captures a new vision.

This illustrates a difference between a vision and a mission statement. A congregation's mission statement will remain the same throughout the life of the congregation while the congregation's vision will change with its circumstances. A change in pastors, new immigration to the neighborhood, shifting cultural norms and values, the cries of new generations will all call for the congregation to reevaluate its vision.

If the pastor and the congregation have not attended to the matter of vision the community will be consigned to wandering in the desert. Every aspect of the congregation's life will suffer. Christian education will lack focus. Worship will lose energy. Leaders will be difficult to find and unenthusiastic when they are found. The congregation will stagnate and begin to decline. Visionary leadership is essential to dynamic, cutting-edge congregations.

This matter of vision is so critical to the life of a group of believers that all congregations will have a de facto vision of their ministry whether they are conscious of it or not. Vision can form and operate without our awareness. Some congregations envision themselves as a museum to the glory days of the past while others see themselves as a sentinel standing guard against the evils of the outside world.

Biblical examples

As in all other matters of faith and life, the Bible is the source for clarifying our understanding of the nature of visionary leadership. We can see vision at work within three of the central stories of Scripture: Moses, Paul, and Jesus. In these narratives, which are not normally associated with the prophetic speeches of the biblical prophets, we find that element too long overlooked among Christians, namely, the need for vision in their leadership. Using these three examples, congregational leaders can build the skills necessary to construct a vision that propels the congregation toward its hoped-for future.

Moses

No doubt many examples of mission and vision can be found in the Scriptures but perhaps none is told in such exquisite detail as the story of Moses and the children of Israel. The journey from Mount Sinai to the threshold of the promised land is the central salvation event of the Old Testament. It is also a profound lesson for leaders who want to understand the biblically distinctive character of mission and vision and the relationship between them. This is also a classic biblical story of a turnaround congregation.

Here in the story of Moses leading the nation of Israel, we see the genesis of vision born in the personal encounter with the living God. We walk alongside Moses as he meets violent opposition from within his own people and from without. We watch Moses' temptation to become infected with negativity of the naysayers, some of whom by their own lack of faith will be left behind as the vision bearers move forward. And finally, we discover the visionary does not always live to see the vision achieved.

Visionary leadership is born in the personal encounter with the living God. It is not a half-baked idea from the leader, arising out of dreams of glory or fame. It is not copied from the successes of other congregations that have been blessed by God and are transformed into national cathedrals. It cannot even be transferred from congregation to congregation when a pastor moves to a new congregation.

In the story of Moses, we see that it was God who initiated the vision by appearing "to him in a flame of fire out of a bush" (Exodus 3:2). In this awesome moment God spoke to Moses (Exodus 3:7) and laid out the compelling picture of the future that remained constant throughout the remainder of Moses' career: "The LORD said, 'I have indeed seen the misery of my people in Egypt. I have heard them crying out because of their slave drivers, and I am concerned about their suffering. So I have come down to rescue them from the hand of the Egyptians and to bring them up out of that land into a good and spacious land, a land flowing with milk and honey'" (NIV).

This is a continuation of the promise made to Abraham many generations before (Genesis 12:1-3; 13:15-17; 15:5,7,18-21; 17:2-8; 22:17-18; and 24:60). It is the same promise repeated to Isaac (Genesis 26:2-4) and to Jacob (Genesis 28:3-4). This Abrahamic covenant is God's unchanging mission. Though the circumstances of God's people changed (they were in bondage in Egypt) the mission of God remained the same. The vision God gave to Moses was specifically tailored to that unique moment in that particular context—the need to be delivered from bondage to enter the promised land.

God's overall mission expressed in the Abrahamic covenant did not change. God still desired that the descendants of Abraham be a blessing and that "all peoples on earth will be blessed through" them (Genesis 12:3 NIV). The Abrahamic covenant was threatened by the centuries-long bondage in

Egypt. Through these particular historical circumstances, God's intention to bless the nations was moved forward. God granted Moses a vision of release from captivity to establishment in the promised land. The vision for mission was to get from point A to point B, not just in terms of geography but, more important, in terms of advancing God's purpose for the children of Israel.

Throughout the narrative of the exodus notice that the vision belonged to God. It was God's future, the inbreaking of the kingdom of God. It was God alone who held the future. Through revelation by vision, God motivated servants to work toward that future reality. This is an essential point to remember throughout the long and difficult days that will inevitably come in seeking to turn a congregation around. It is critical that the congregation never loses sight of this divine reality: the vision belongs to God. It will be easy to confuse the resulting success of the vision with the congregation's efforts or abilities. We are simply stewards of the vision of the coming kingdom of God; we are not the owners of the vision. We are privileged to be workers in God's vineyard.

Early in the congregation's study phase it is imperative for the congregation to wrestle with God in prayer, seeking God's vision for the future. Prayers can be for illumination to see God's vision for the ministry of the congregation in its unique historical context. What is important to note is that the vision for the congregation cannot come from any one member or group of members. Nor can leaders dream up some creative vision and then ask for God's blessing upon it. It is God's future. God already has a destination in mind, and as God reminded Isaiah: "For my thoughts are not your thoughts, nor are your ways my ways, says the LORD" (Isaiah 55:8). As for our part, Paul was not only poetic but correct when he wrote, "For now we see in a mirror, dimly, but then we will see face to face" (1 Corinthians 13:12).

Stephen Covey in his book *Principle-Centered Leadership,*[1] suggests that the second habit of leaders is to "begin with the end in mind." Covey describes this by saying, "I have created the future in my mind. I can see it, and I can imagine what it will be like."[2] Christian leaders pull up the floorboards of Covey's insight to locate the foundation of true vision. We do not create God's future; only God creates God's future. The story of Moses teaches this lesson in epic style.

From the story of the exodus we learn about mission and vision for our congregations and ministries. From pastor to pastor, from one church board to the next, from era to era the mission of God for the congregation remains the same. God's love is to be made known to all the world. God has created the church to preach, teach, baptize, and evangelize. This mission bridges time, culture, border, and race.

Vision is distinct from, but a servant of, mission. In each era of the congregation's life a new vision is given by God to meet the unique challenges of mission in that time and in that place. When the circumstances of the congregation change—neighborhood shifts, new pastor, influx of new members, relocation—a renewed vision from God will be needed. The congregation will continue to preach, teach, and baptize—its mission—but how it specializes to move forward in that mission will need to be adapted.

Jesus

In reading the Gospel accounts of Jesus we discover Jesus' mission and vision. Jesus revealed his mission to the crowds who followed him from Capernaum: "I must proclaim the good news of the kingdom of God to the other cities also; for I was sent for this purpose" (Luke 4:43). Jesus was about his Father's business in proclaiming the coming of the kingdom of God. This was his single-minded mission. It is this mission that continued still as he sent forth disciples to "go therefore and make disciples." With each new disciple baptized and taught the kingdom comes a little closer. The mission continues past the earthly life of Jesus.

The vision that compelled Jesus forward toward this mission was just as single-minded. Jesus responded to Peter with the other disciples within earshot: "The Son of Man must undergo great suffering, and be rejected by the elders, chief priests, and scribes, and be killed, and on the third day be raised" (Luke 9:22). This was the specific future that God had in store for Jesus for the purpose of advancing God's mission, Jesus' future destination of the last day. The vision God gave to Jesus was to commence God's redemptive activity through death on the cross and three days later to rise again. (For Jesus' understanding of the vision given him, see Mark 10:32-34.)

Paul

The epistles of Paul provide further valuable illustration of Christian mission and vision. Paul was clearly a man on a mission. After Paul's dramatic Damascus road experience, Ananias, Paul's early benefactor, told him of Jesus' commission for his life: "for you will be his witness to all the world of what you have seen and heard" (Acts 22:15). This mission is directly linked to the mission of Jesus to bring about the kingdom through bearing witness to all the world. Paul was called to be a part of God's ongoing redemptive activity to reconcile the world unto God. This was his mission.

Within this overarching mission was the specificity of a vision from Christ. In his address before Agrippa, Paul talked about the vision given to him. Paul recounted the words of Jesus to him: "I will rescue you from your people and from the Gentiles—to whom I am sending you to open their eyes so that they may turn from darkness to light" (Acts 26:17-18). In his letter to the Galatians, Paul was even clearer that he was sent specifically to the uncircumcised while Peter was sent to the circumcised. Both Peter and Paul shared the same mission, to go and make disciples, but each had a unique vision to use their particular gifts with a specific group of people. Paul's God-given vision for mission was to preach to the Gentiles the good news of Jesus Christ.

Knowing your context

As you begin the study phase, invite the congregation to work hard to avoid arriving prematurely at a vision for mission. The next stage of the study phase, that of "Understanding the Congregation" detailed in the next chapter, will shed light on what it is that Christ wants of your congregation. Setting a foundation of common understanding about mission and vision is only the first step. Getting an accurate picture of the current reality and context of your congregation is essential to discovering God's vision, which will turn around your situation. This self-discovery is the subject of chapter five.

Reflection questions

1. Locate your congregation's mission statement. Reflect on this statement in light of Scripture and this chapter's definitions of mission and vision.

2. What visions are operating unnoticed in your congregation right now?

Notes

1.Stephen R. Covey, *Principle-Centered Leadership* (New York: Simon & Schuster, 1990).

2. Ibid, 42–43.

5 Turning toward Health: Study
Understanding the Congregation

Make it thy business to know thyself,
which is the most difficult lesson in the world.

Miguel de Cervantes
***Don Quixote*, chapter 42**

You arrive at the doctor's office after putting off this appointment for far too long. It's time for a complete history and physical with a doctor you have never seen before. You are led into a tight room where the nurse takes your vital signs: pulse, blood pressure, and temperature, followed by height and weight (ouch!). While you wait for the doctor, the nurse asks you to fill out a form indicating your past medical history. "Have you ever had any of the following diseases?" the form demands. "Any family history of these illnesses?" The list seems endless.

When the doctor arrives she begins to review your checklist as well as the notes about your vital signs made by the nurse. She inquires further into your history, asking for more detail about the items you checked. More notes go into the chart for future reference.

When the doctor has completed her exam she sends you down the hall to the lab. Some blood is drawn and a urine sample is taken for analysis. It will be a few days before the results are in. The doctor promises she will call you with the results. If anything shows up, a follow-up visit will be scheduled to determine what treatment might be required. Perhaps just a prescription or two; maybe a procedure or even surgery will be required. In any case, the goal of this entire examination process is to assess your current health and, if necessary, to restore you to that wonderful balance of life.

This is a description of a routine history and physical from the patient's perspective. The physician has been trained to follow a standardized procedure, seeking the chief complaint and then assessing the history of the present illness. Family history comes next, followed by habits such as smoking, and then a list of any current medications or allergies. Your physician then takes a social history to learn more about your lifestyle and who you are emotionally. The doctor searches for any illness in the major organ systems of the body. All this is charted, along with a general description of you, followed by an assessment and plan for treatment.

The majority of the study phase in congregational renewal is similar. It is time for a wellness check of the church. The difference is that the patient and the physician are one and the same. Regardless, an objective and thorough examination of your unique health using the criteria outlined in chapters one and two is called for. A physician cannot give a prognosis without first making a diagnosis.

In the case of a history and physical exam of the congregation, however, it is the diagnosis that is dreaded. Organizational systems by their very nature resist at all costs the diagnosis of their system-wide dysfunctions. The problem is even worse for Christian congregations having the attitude that inside the church everything is just fine.

Chief complaint

Something has caused the congregation to contemplate entering into this renewal process. Perhaps it is a gnawing sense of slow erosion or maybe a glaringly obvious free fall in attendance and giving. Whatever the case, it is important to begin by putting into writing why it is that the congregation is undertaking this process. As George Barna observed in his research on turn-around congregations, a critical component was that the church must recognize the crisis.[1] Drafting a statement of the chief complaint is a first step in this recognition.

No one person's perspective will be adequate. It will take a summary of opinions to grasp the depth of the current dissatisfaction within the congregation. The vision team might consider interviews with staff and leaders of the various ministries of the congregation. To this end, a single questionnaire administered personally by a member of the vision team would serve to dig out the information to draft a statement of the initial complaint. A general questionnaire mailed to the entire membership is discouraged. In general, such questionnaires are very difficult to draft and allow people to take undeserved pot shots without personal accountability. More often than not they discourage rather than encourage.

Once completed, this statement of the congregation's present status will, from this point on, serve as a baseline for the congregation as it grows in understanding itself. Undoubtedly, this initial statement will seem simplistic once the entire study phase is completed and the totality of the congregation's difficulties is uncovered.

History of present problems

Next the vision team proceeds to uncover the hidden elements to the congregation's dilemma. This can be accomplished by reviewing the seven congregational health criteria outlined in chapters one and two. Here the vision team turns to the congregation to ask them the question, Is our congregation healthy? The vision team can use its best judgment in how to gather the congregation for discussion of questions such as:

- Organization. Do we have an organization patterned for the mission we seek to accomplish? Does it fit our vision?
- Growth. Are we growing? If not, why not? What invisible barriers are keeping unchurched people away?
- Movement. Where have we been going? Is that where we want to go?
- Transformation. Are lives being changed here? Are even long-time members continuing to be transformed by the gospel?
- Sensitivity. Have we really listened to our churched and

unchurched neighbors and contemporary culture? Are we out of touch?
- Adaptation. Are we following tradition because it still serves our mission and vision or for tradition's sake? Are we truly adaptive to new models for ministry?
- Reproduction. How are we really doing in growing a new generation of disciples?

It will be a matter of considerable grace to address these problems forthrightly without inflicting further damage to anyone. To not honestly address the issues that no one wants to talk about will scuttle all the work to follow. A turn around simply will never take place without dealing with these concerns now. The Christian church above all ought to be a place where we can tell the truth in love.

To accomplish such a health assessment the vision team might use the skills of other congregational members with vocations in social work, counseling, or in the medical profession. Invite these persons to help design a method for addressing these issues in the most humane manner possible. Professionals in these and similar vocations have invaluable expertise to lend to the vision team and might be excellent leaders to facilitate this portion of the process.

Family history

One hopes that the congregation has a larger and longer history than the history of its most recent decline. The vision team, in responding to its commissioning goal of preparing the background research the congregation needs to make its decision, can assemble a representation of this larger history. Graphics of worship attendance, membership, and giving displayed on large charts can be helpful tools during important congregational forums. A listing of all the pastors and other key staff and their lengths of service might also be helpful information for the vision team to gather. Trends here might enable the congregation to discover important information about itself and the effect it has had on its ministry personnel.

Another helpful piece in the diagnosis is to compile an abbreviated version of the congregation's history. This brief history should narrate the founding vision of the congregation and all successive visions. A historical time line highlighting key events in the congregation's life story not only is instructive to newer members but also serves to remind the longtime members of the historic mission and vision of the congregation.

Context and environment

It is very easy to live in a community for decades and overlook the changes that have taken place. This is the case in many a neighborhood where a congregation has plateaued or declined. Years of maintaining the same shopping habits, social networks, and driving patterns have a way of insulating us from the changes taking place in the community. Living in the same house can, over time, leave one unaware of the changes in the cost of housing. No longer having school-aged children can leave one ignorant of who is moving into the community and who is moving out. It would be surprising for a congregation that is more than thirty years old if the neighborhood were the same as when the founding members first organized the congregation.

Now is the time to reexamine the neighborhood of the church. In this modern information age, there are a number of excellent resources for gathering current demographic data on a particular service area. Many denominations can gather this information for member congregations, or a congregation can hire a consulting service to supply it with census-style information on the community. Local chambers of commerce can be good sources of information. The congregation needs to think like a business considering a move into the locality. What would it need to know?

One strategy might be to ask several members who are new to the community to share their perspectives on the ministry of the congregation. The congregation can be invited to gather to listen carefully without attempting to "correct" these new members perceptions. Another method might be to encourage members to stop at some local gas stations or restaurants and ask the locals what they know about "Faith Church" (substitute your congregation's name) as if the members had no prior knowledge of the church. Such information gathering will facilitate direct learning about how the congregation is perceived by the community and what impact it is having in that place.

Discovering the congregation's culture

Congregations are a subculture unto themselves; they possess all the characteristics of a culture. Edgar Schein is a professor of management at the Massachusetts Institute of Technology and an expert in organizational behavior. Schein defines culture as "A pattern of shared basic assumptions that the group learned as it solved its problems of external adaptation and internal integration, that has worked well enough to be considered valid and, therefore, to be taught to new members as the correct way to perceive, think, and feel in relation to those problems."[2] In other words, all groupings of people have a set of shared assumptions that lie unexamined but still are consciously and unconsciously passed to newcomers. This is culture.

Schein argues that there are three levels of culture. The first is that of *artifacts*, that is to say, "visible organizational structures and processes." The annual lutefisk dinner might be an artifact of a congregation founded by Norwegian immigrants. The fact that this artifact survives indicates some continuing emotional ties to this past.

The second, and deeper, level is that of *espoused values* of the group. These values are a direct reflection of the original values of the founding members of the group, however long ago that was. These are values at the conscious level as opposed to the next category. An example of an espoused value in a congregation might be a high priority for worship, which reflects the gifts and emphases of the founding pastor who instilled in the congregation a strong value for high quality in worship.

Finally, beneath the prior two levels lie *basic assumptions.* These are the true values of the group that operate so implicitly no one needs to discuss them. Schein states that anyone in the group who took issue with these values would be dismissed as crazy. An example in a congregational culture might be the congregation that assumes that "Christians don't have conflicts" and so open conflict is avoided at all costs.

Uncovering the cultural artifacts is often like interpreting dreams. Only when one has lived long enough in a congregation's culture do these begin to have meaning. Espoused values take time to collect, less so if founding members can be interviewed about the early days of the congregation. As for the basic assumptions, this is altogether a more difficult task. It is also where energy needs to be placed in order to significantly alter the course of the congregation.

Schein asserts that basic assumptions are those suppositions we don't confront or debate. As a result, they are extremely difficult to bring to the surface to examine and possibly change our thinking. Such learning is difficult because reexamining basic assumptions temporarily destabilizes the structure and pattern of our thoughts and behavior, and this causes great anxiety.[3] We are not surprised to discover that examining our unconscious assumptions about the group to which we belong can produce tension. Change is painful.

Kenneth Mitchell in his book *Multiple Staff Ministries* offers a poignant, if not painful, illustration of why it is so important to uncover these basic assumptions of the congregation's culture. He describes a particular congregation that was characterized in 1955 as a "problem church" in its denomination. Thirty years later, during which there was a 97 percent turnover in members and four pastors, the congregation was still a problem church. In spite of the years and the fact that less than twenty members remained from 1955, the issues were identical to 1955.[4] Unknowingly the congregation had passed its basic assumptions to several generations of new members, thus carrying forward its systemic dysfunctions.

As one can see, it is critical to search for these unspoken cultural clues in order to understand their power over the congregation. Often some of these are the invisible barriers that hold a congregation back from where it wants to go. If these basic assumptions can be brought forward to consciousness, they can then be examined and modified, if need be. Other basic assumptions may, in fact, be assets.

Social history

A physician, when performing a history and physical, takes notes on the patient's social history. This is also a helpful practice in this study phase, especially if the congregation has a new pastor. This social history reveals the natural constituencies that make up the structural system of the group. An excellent method to gather this social history is through hosting cottage meetings within the congregation.

A cottage meeting is a gathering of ten to fifteen members in an informal setting. The aim is to allow the membership to tell its story while the facilitator gathers important sociological data on the history of the congregation and the current make-up of its social units. To do this, the vision team organizes enough cottage meetings to accommodate about half of its average worship attendance (this number represents the core of active members in most congregations). Figuring the average worship attendance divided by two and then divided again by twelve should produce a rough estimate of how many meetings it might take. (Congregations with more than five hundred people present for worship will need to work out another formula to reach its opinion leaders in a reasonable number of meetings.)

The vision team seeks volunteers to host the meetings in their homes or, less desirably, at the church's facility. Then, and this is the critical move, members select which cottage meetings to attend, rather than leaders assigning members to groups. The facilitators from the vision team will quickly get an idea of who naturally groups together. One attendee at the cottage meeting serves as the recorder, telling the group that the vision team is attempting to build a historical time line of the congregation's life together. The facilitator simply listens as the group responds the following three topics.

- Recount the history of this congregation.
- What do you dream for the future?
- What does a newcomer need to know about our congregation?

As people respond to the first topic about recounting the history of this congregation, it is important for the facilitator to resist giving any more specificity to this general query. Some groups will go three years back while others speak of events thirty years ago. Some groups will mention every wonderful fellowship event while others speak only of the fights the congregation has endured. What each gathering chooses to tell and how far back they choose to go provides valuable data to draw upon to help construct the congregation's systems and coalitions.

With the second question it is again important for the facilitator to resist granting any more definition to the question. The facilitator listens to whatever comes up, as the recorder plots the future timeline delineated by the group. They may speak of paying off the old debt still maintained by the congregation or they may speak of hoping to improve Sunday school. Leaders should listen for any early wins that the congregation has long dreamed of accomplishing but lacked the coordinated leadership to complete. These will be superb additions to the plan created in the next phase, setting up the congregation for early success.

Finally, the gathering solves the riddle: What does a newcomer need to know about our congregation? This open-ended question will reveal all manner of valuable information about the group's basic assumptions and espoused values. It will also speak volumes about what holds this particular group of people together. For example, do they value more social outreach ministries or would they like to see more contemporary worship? Armed with the data from these cottage meetings the vision team constructs a social history, testing its validity with the general membership.

Review of systems

The physician in examining her patient looks at the systems of the body; for example, the immune system, the nervous system, the digestive system. Each of these systems is, in reality, a complex interrelationship of various organs and their functions working together for a common purpose. In the past thirty years, a similar type of thinking has been developed for looking at groups of people in the same systematic fashion. Human beings too, it seems, interact with one another in complex interrelationships that form systems.

Peter Senge in *The Fifth Discipline* defines *systems thinking* as "seeing interrelationships rather than linear cause-effect chains, and seeing processes of change rather than snapshots."[5]

Let us take the example of Trinity Church, which was in a numerical decline for nine years. In calling a new pastor, the system was changed, resulting in a new growth pattern. The sudden new growth, however, immediately produced a new set of problems. Why? Use of systems thinking enables us to determine the answer.

What was different in the system? A new pastor was introduced into the system, thus the system was no longer the same as before. From this new pastor and congregational leaders sprang *new ideas* that produced a *new vision* and that resulted in *growth* (see figure 5.1). Given this information, it would be logical to assume that if the new pastor just worked harder at spinning that wheel of change, the congregation would continue to grow. Right? Yet systems do not work this way. Senge

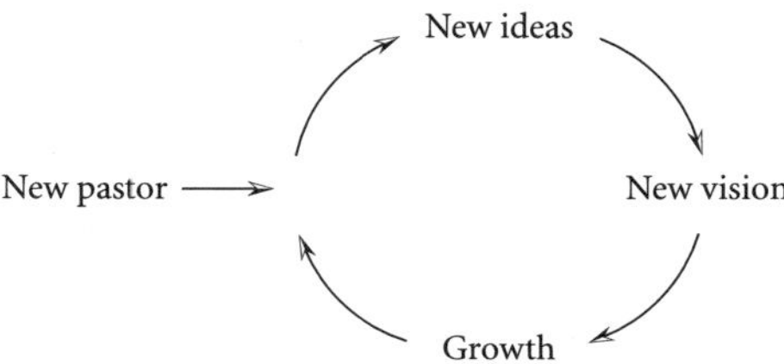

Fig. 5.1

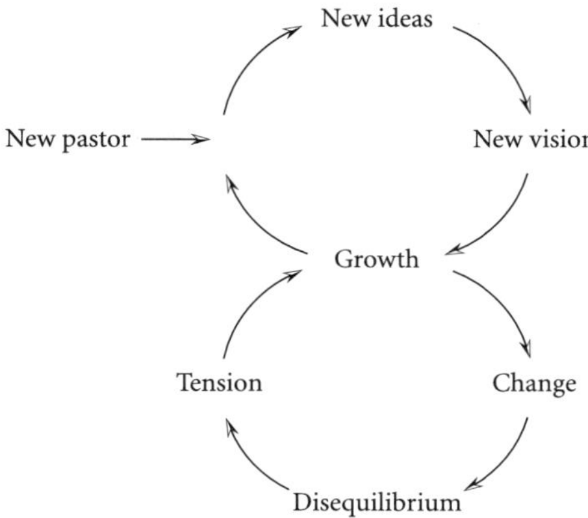

Fig. 5.2

teaches us to apply Newton's third law of motion: To every action there is always opposed an equal reaction.[6]

Inevitably the force of this first wheel of change produced an equal reaction as illustrated in figure 5.2. *Growth* produced *change* that in turn produced a *disequilibrium* in the congregation, which created *tension* that counteracted *growth.* However, this was not the only countervailing force in the changed system. Figure 5.3 illustrates how the *new vision* prompted *people to talk about vision* resulting in the *recognition of disparities of vision* among the membership, which created *tension*, which acted against the *new vision.* Further, in figure 5.4 we see how *change* produced *new programs* and this created the *need for more space*, again resulting in *tension* that acted to resist *change.*

Such systems thinking illustrates the complexity of congregational dynamics and reveals a hidden barrier to growth. Matters are not as simple as they may first appear! Yet, once these dynamics are flushed out, potential intervention can be devised. Inventor and mathematician Archimedes once said, "give me a lever long enough . . . and single-handed I can move the world."[7]

Knowing where to apply the lever in the case of Trinity can enable the congregation to continue growing. The technique is to decelerate the countervailing forces rather than attempt to

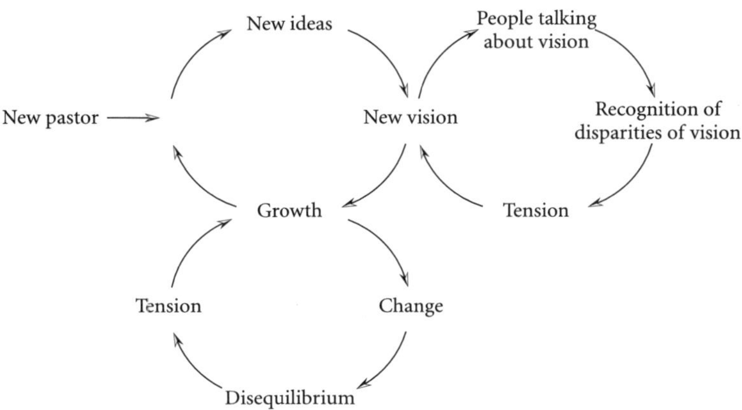

Fig. 5.3

increase the growth forces themselves. Strategically applying a lever of intervention in the right spots (marked by the dark arrows in figure 5.5) slows down some of the *change* that will alleviate some of the *disequilibrium* and consequently some of the *tension* that held up *growth*. Similarly, in the other parts of the system, if a cohesive congregational vision could be achieved, then folks would not feel so much tension over the *disparity of vision*. Also, if Trinity could create new *space* for programs, there would be less friction against *change*. Leveraging change in these initially hidden arenas will accomplish the sought-after goal of continued missional growth.

Consulting a specialist

In congregations with severe, chronic, and unresolved conflict, an impartial, outside consultant or consulting team may be the only solution. Such a congregation, stuck in a destructive downward cycle, lacks the internal motivation or resources to move forward and heal itself. However, before an outside consultant is brought in, the congregation will need some basic agreements among members. Speed Leas, himself an expert conflict consultant, offers advice on this congregational con-

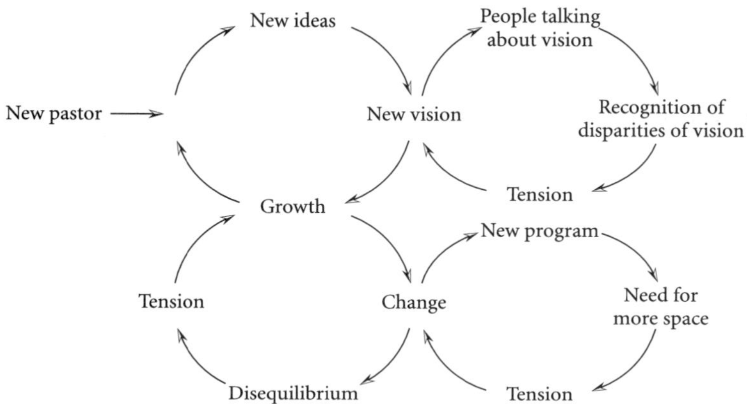

Fig. 5.4

tract in his book, *Church Fights: Managing Conflict in the Local Church*.[8]

Leas advocates the congregation begin by negotiating how the congregation will act and interact with the consultant. The second stage of Leas's proposal is to decide on a conflict resolution process, goals, and a timeline.

Above all, the congregation must agree to listen carefully to the observations of the consultant. Inevitably, once the consultant uncovers the hidden and painful sources of the church's dysfunction, the body will recoil and reject the consultant's counsel. The more accurate the counsel, the more violently the congregational system will reject the findings. Advance agreement by the congregation to receive this specialist's diagnosis enables the congregation to take the necessary medicine.

General description

A general description of the congregation is now assembled and written for the purpose of clarifying what everyone assumes is obvious. As a fictional example, a congregation might draft the following: "St. Mary's is a forty-five-year-old congregation established to serve the burgeoning exurb of Hilldale. Its origi-

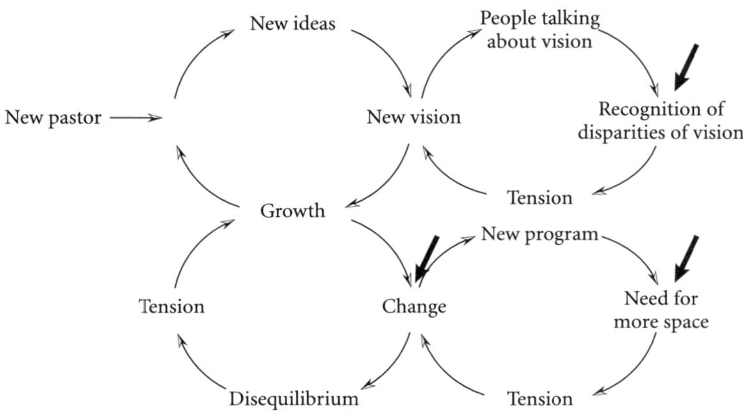

Fig. 5.5

nal mission was to plant a congregation of its denomination within this new growth area. The present vision of the congregation is to reach young families through strong youth and family ministry, though the neighborhood has now aged and the number of young families with children is declining. St. Mary's has a history of conflict that has caused it to lose significant membership over the past five years." The description could go on with further specifics, but it will need to be brief (one page maximum) for it to be usable.

Once drafted, the congregation can use this general description to solidify in everyone's mind a unified set of perceptions about the congregation's current status. Such consensus creates a common understanding before the next stage of the turn around.

Assessment

Now the congregation has the information it needs to fully devise a plan for turning itself around. This final assessment of all that has been learned through the study phase can be carefully written and assembled. This will become a part of the congregation's history, as well as have many other uses. Future leaders, new to the congregation, will find this assessment an invaluable aid to knowing what the membership has been through.

This unflinchingly honest assessment concludes the study phase. By this point the congregation will have experienced many new internal dynamics that will prepare it for the third stage of the process: the plan phase. It is time to move forward.

Reflection questions

1. Who among your newest members could you ask for honest perspectives of your church?

2. Reflect on the subconscious values of your congregation. How can you check out your perceptions?

3. How would you respond to the three cottage meeting topics: Recount the history of the congregation; What do you dream of for the future? and What does a newcomer need to know about our congregation?

Notes

1. Barna, *Turnaround Churches*, 58.

2. Edgar H. Schein, *Organizational Culture and Leadership*, 2nd ed. (San Francisco: Jossey-Bass Publishers, 1992), 12.

3. Ibid., 22.

4. Kenneth R. Mitchell, *Multiple Staff Ministries* (Philadelphia: Westminster Press, 1988), 36.

5. Senge, *Fifth Discipline,* 73.

6. David Halliday and Robert Resnick, *Physics*, combined 3rd ed. (New York: John Wiley and Sons, 1978), 79.

7. Senge, *Fifth Discipline*, 13.

8. Speed Leas, *Church Fights: Managing Conflict in the Local Church* (Philadelphia: Westminster Press, 1973), 78–79.

6 Turning toward Health: Plan
Kindling a Shared Vision

An invasion of armies can be resisted,
but not an idea whose time has come.

Victor Hugo,
***Histoire d'un Crime*, conclusion, 1852**

The biblical story of Nehemiah is more than just a great story for the flannel boards of Sunday school classrooms. It is also a profound lesson on the power of vision to rebuild a congregation of people through a common purpose. This powerful vision was born in Nehemiah's personal encounter with God. Yet, it was not Nehemiah's vision alone. Throughout the story we learn that Nehemiah was a master at kindling a shared vision. He gathered officials of the Jewish priests, nobles, and the workers and captivated their hearts and minds by the vision that began in his prayers. "Let us start building!" was the spontaneous and enthusiastic response from these leaders (Nehemiah 2:18).

The vision, however, was not to rebuild the walls of Jerusalem; that was its method. The real vision in the book of Nehemiah was God's vision to rebuild the people of God from a scattered and oppressed people into a unified nation that feared and loved God. This was Nehemiah's motivation as we see in Nehemiah 1:8-9. The completion of the wall reveals this more distinctly. Nehemiah took a census (chapter 7) and Jerusalem was renewed because of what God had done. This was God's larger vision. Through the conflict involved in rebuilding the walls of Jerusalem, the people grew in their trust of each other and of God. They also revived their covenant with

God. The unity of the children of Israel was renewed like no time in the prior three centuries.

In celebration, the priest Ezra recalled God's mighty acts as he read from the book of Deuteronomy before the assembly of the people. As one, the people were filled with great joy (see 8:12ff, especially verse 17). They generously sacrificed their tithes and offerings (chapter 10) to return what God had first given them, giving up silver and gold along with priceless family heirlooms. In the end, they were united in the same cry: "We will not neglect the house of our God" (10:39).

Shared vision, as the story of Nehemiah reveals, is the essential ingredient needed to accomplish a congregational turn around. Only a vivid mental picture of the future God desires, shared among the majority of the membership, will propel the congregation through its status quo. No single program or quick fix will suffice. Attempting to address a single issue or perceived weakness without a comprehensive vision for the future will result in reinforcing the congregation's perception of itself as a failure. Only shared vision revealed by God's divine grace will capture the hearts and minds of the membership, transforming the congregation for mission.

Achieving this shared vision, however, is a delicate art. And, as with any art form, there is no formula. Instead, a shared vision is a deliberate, collective listening to God's guidance toward the future. Such listening happens only through faith in Christ. The goal of the plan phase of the turn-around process is to kindle this shared vision. Without it, the plan and actions that arise will only be fingers in the dike. Nor will the energy, momentum, and forward movement necessary to reverse the inertia of decline ever be generated.

The study phase, when completed by the congregation, produces a common understanding of the challenges faced by the membership. A mutual vocabulary is established along with a shared set of criteria for determining what a healthy congregation will look like. With these vital steps accomplished, the people of God are ready to listen carefully to find God's unique vision for their mission.

Design review

At this point the vision team needs to reevaluate the design set forth at the outset of the turn around. By now the team has a very clear sense of how the congregation has approached the task at hand. The vision team can gauge the trust level built up through these months of studying the issues together. It can assess the level of conflict and tension the process has generated. The study phase has empowered the membership to evaluate the healthiness of the body.

Further reflection guides the vision team in refining the plan phase. Questions such as the following might be examined:

- How have the methods employed in the study phase worked? What was more helpful—congregational forums or some other method?
- Can these methods be revised based on what has been learned thus far in the process ?
- What about the mood of the congregation? Is it on the upswing with positive momentum and excitement toward a new future? Or is unaddressed conflict brewing a spiteful poison throughout the membership and the community?
- Is the community beyond the membership hearing about what is happening? What is their reaction?

These are just a few of the assessments the vision team makes at this stage. Answers to these questions enable the team to refine its early outline of the plan phase before initiating it among the congregation. An exhaustive plan phase involves two distinct stages. The first is the actual process of building a congregationally based vision for mission. The second is mapping the detail necessary for moving ahead toward the newfound vision.

A congregationally based vision

Viktor Frankl once said that one doesn't invent one's mission, one detects it.[1] The first stage of the plan phase involves the congregation's detection of God's vision for its future mission.

It is the responsibility of the vision team to gather as many willing members as they can to participate and then to create a method in which the congregation can work together to build a shared vision.

It is altogether too tempting to skip this stage of building a vision and just get right to work on piecing together a comprehensive plan. This is a fatal mistake. The most important leadership axiom for a turn-around church is "shoot the biggest bear in camp first." In other words, address the most critical need first. Vision is that biggest bear, the most critical need. Without it, there is no point to any further planning. It would be like framing and roofing a house before the foundation was laid. All the work would be for naught.

This is precisely why so many contemporary books, ministry programs, and seminars are rejected as simple gimmicks. Contemporary music, worship drama, youth ministry, pastoral care programs, and the like are all well and good. The promoters of these ideas are certainly well-intentioned and truly believe their ideas are of value. And they are! However, the one missing piece is that congregations that have found these programs so effective are congregations whose vision it is to reach a demographic group through music or to specialize in youth ministry. Vision is the difference. The program is the detailed road map of how to aim for the target the vision creates.

The Lord spoke through the prophet Habakkuk promising a vision if we are patient enough to wait for it. "Write the vision; make it plain on tablets, so that a runner may read it. For there is still a vision for the appointed time; it speaks of the end, and does not lie. If it seems to tarry, wait for it; it will surely come, it will not delay" (Habakkuk 2:2b-3). Such is God's way in the world. God still leads the church. God will be the author of this foundational vision for mission, for only God can transform the deepest core of the membership's unexpressed dreams for its future and align human will with God's divine will.

Three steps will be needed to detect God's vision: discussion, deliberation, and finally decision. The congregation will find it helpful to discuss the ideas derived from the study phase and then will need some manner of deliberating with one another. The most difficult facet is in finally deciding on one vision over other possible contenders.

Discussion

The congregation's discussion of vision begins with an understanding of the three levels of vision. In any large group, in our case a Christian congregation, there can be three levels of communal vision.[2] The lowest and most common level is that of *competing vision*. In this bottom level there are shared visions, but the entire congregation does not share the same vision. A single constituency, or even a coalition of constituencies, holds fast to a particular vision for the congregation. This vision, since it is not shared by the entire membership, is at odds with the vision of other constituencies. These visions are mutually exclusive. They cannot both be fulfilled and as such they compete with one another for validity.

For example, one constituency may have a vision of the church as a museum to the past glory days. Its ideal future is for the church to recreate those wonderful days so lovingly remembered. At the very same time, another constituency of members may hold to a vision of a seeker-friendly worship center that uses the latest in contemporary worship to draw the unchurched from the community to hear the gospel in a fresh way. It is readily apparent that these two visions will compete with one another for scarce resources of time, money, and leadership from within the membership.

The next level of vision within large groups is that of *cooperative visions*. Here again there are shared vision among portions of the congregation but it is not pervasive throughout the entire body. This level of vision requires varying constituencies within the larger membership to cooperate with one another to move forward their particular vision. Cooperative visions need delicate political diplomacy to survive. Constituencies or coalitions of constituencies must negotiate with constituencies having altogether different visions. Each subgroup of the congregation must compromise some of its particular vision.

Picture, for example, the youth ministry constituency made up of youth and young families who must cooperate with the old guard constituency of the congregation. The youth constituency wants a youth room to fulfill part of its vision for the congregation to be a place where the community's youth can hang out and hear the transforming power of the gospel. The old guard have loved and cared for the church's building since they built it and their vision is to preserve this place intact for future generations. The cooperative vision created is a mutual pact in which the youth constituency agrees to finance and maintain the youth room within certain limits of decor and use. The youth constituency compromised some of its future and the old guard sacrificed some of its hoped-for future. The result is a vision somewhat different than each group previously desired.

Finally, the highest level of vision is the *supraordinate vision*. In this vision there is complete unity among the entire membership. The term *supraordinate* implies a vision that brings about an order transcending the competing and cooperative needs of the individual constituencies that make up the congregation. In spite of these differences among the constituent subgroups, all can pledge their allegiance to a vision that rises above their natural competitions and compromises.

The vision of God seen in the book of Nehemiah is an excellent example of a supraordinate vision. Every faction among the returning exiles, whether nobles or peasants, farmers or merchants, leaders or common folk, could pledge its allegiance to this vision that transcended partisan politics.

Detecting such supraordinate visions out of the competing and cooperative visions is no easy or quick task. The vision team is charged with finding a method by which the membership can discuss vision in such a manner as to detect a supraordinate vision from God. The vision team's major goal is to facilitate the congregation's discussion in such a way that congregation members can discover this for themselves.

But the question remains: Just how does a congregation of believers detect the vision God has for the future at this moment in history? The question, put simply, is: How do one hundred or 350 or even four thousand individuals simultaneously detect the same vision from God in order to move forward in faith?

One must first recognize that the detection of the vision is already in progress throughout the study phase. The data derived from the initial phase of the turn around is the initial detection of God's vision. Lifting out common threads from the study phase sheds light on God's guidance. What recurring themes were discussed? Were there any compelling images or metaphors that stood out from among the rest? What nuggets of pure wisdom caught the imagination of others? These gathered themes, images, metaphors, and bits of wisdom are the raw data from which the supraordinate vision arises.

The discussion of these common threads can now be focused more clearly, using a technique called the APA brainstorming method.[3] APA is an acronym for *a*chieve, *p*rotect, and *a*void. This method commences with the facilitator inviting those gathered to arrange the ideas and information lifted from the study phase into three categories: those things the congregation wishes to achieve, protect, and avoid.

The goal is to discern potential visions by listing everything the congregation hopes to achieve, protect, and avoid. After sorting the prior ideas into the three categories the congregation adds other brainstormed thoughts to those previously assembled. A lengthy list is generated and recorded on flip charts that are then posted on the wall. It is surprising how the list generates intriguing new ideas never before considered. Here it becomes more obvious how the Holy Spirit draws out the gifts and wisdom of the body of Christ.

Throughout the brainstorming, the group refrains from placing value judgments on the ideas that are generated. This allows the group members to spark ideas off from one another, never knowing which ideas will capture the imagination of the whole group. Laying side-by-side these three categories of achieve, protect, and avoid, the group can then look for common threads running through them.

Those gathered should be invited to take these threads and sketch them into complete, imaginative depictions of potential futures. This process is commonly known as scenario planning. The group members draw out a range of scenarios that have arisen from the information at hand, flesh out each scenario into as vivid a mental picture as possible, and use their imaginations to envision what the future might be like in each scenario.

And next comes the hard part: The group must resist the temptation to choose one. At least not yet. Instead, these scenarios should be circulated among the congregation through multiple means—at worship, in mass mailings, through discussion at existing church programs and ministries—and the staff should mull them over. The congregation's prayers over these alternate scenarios should be solicited. Patience is required. This will take time. A supraordinate vision needs time to ignite in people's hearts before it sweeps through the membership like a fire across the Great Plains. Patience allows the vision to belong to all the people and not to some small group. These scenarios will be informally deliberated among members as they test them out with one another.

Deliberation

Stephen Covey, in *The Seven Habits of Highly Effective People*, lists *synergy* as habit number six. Covey states that "synergy is almost as if a group collectively agrees to subordinate old scripts and to write a new one."[4] Such synergy is needed to deliberate on these alternate scenarios. Synergy propels the congregation forward into prayerful consideration of these ideas. By the grace of God, the entire process to date has created a high trust level among the congregation. A high level of trust serves the members well as they deliberate over potential visions.

It would be altogether too easy to construct a vision that suits the members' own interests instead of God's preferred future. Herein lies the importance of the congregation having done its homework on the surrounding community. God's vision is that through Jesus all things might be reconciled to God (Colossians 1:20). God's vision is to find the one sheep that was lost; not that the lost should be ignored while ninety-nine have their every comfort (Matthew 18:10-14).

In the midst of deliberating over potential visions, the congregation will find it helpful to test these visions. One measuring stick for such testing for a true vision from God is how well it serves God's mission to the lost and lonely of our world who so desperately need God's love. Judging the potential visions by what we know of God's desires for the world from the Scriptures prevents the congregation from self-serving visions.

In these congregational deliberations prayer links the will of each member to the supraordinate will of God who alone holds the entire future. To this end, the vision team might schedule a congregation-wide day of prayer and fasting by coordinating an around-the-clock prayer vigil. Here members are specifically invited to pray for God's guidance. Prayer conforms our will with God's will. Prayer also enables God's power to break down our own selfish desires that we might die to our self-dependency and put our total trust in Christ alone.

The hope of this deliberation stage is that one scenario begins to emerge from among the rest. One vision, whether it is a combination of facets of the previous scenarios or a solitary vision that has begun to ignite passion and enthusiasm among the general membership—an idea whose time has come—is sought. Such a vision will produce some fear and trepidation along with the vibrant energy sought after. This is a natural part of the faith we put in Christ. The old Adam inside us all is far too attached to absolute security and predictability. God, in contrast, leads us to the edge asking us to completely trust.

A remaining complicating factor is adding clarity to this emerging vision. At this point it still looks quite different within the imagination of each member. Here the team does some advance work to craft the vision that has emerged so far. The team might search the membership for people with special gifts in listening and writing. These gifts could be enlisted to hone the vision into a vivid image that can be communicated easily. Once completed, the team presents this honed vision to the congregation to check for clarity and accuracy.

Decision

One of the most difficult things for congregations to do is to make a decision. The pain increases exponentially the more sweeping the change wrought by the decision. Furthermore, the difficulty increases the larger the membership of the congregation becomes until it reaches a threshold where the membership no longer expects to be personally involved in every decision. Thus mega-churches find it easier to make major decisions than do medium-sized congregations.

The key element to congregational decisions lies in deciding beforehand how to decide. Frank discussion about how the congregation will go about making major decisions is essential to a smooth process. It is a matter of wise discernment for the vision team to assess when the congregation is ready to choose a vision. Deciding prematurely is likely to promote a self-centered vision instead of one centered on God, while waiting too long could result in the congregation missing the moment, growing frustrated, and abandoning the process. The best outcome is one where no formal decision is necessary. The most effective and compelling visions are those that produce a spontaneous burst of commitment from the members, just as we see in the story of Nehemiah.

But what if that does not happen? One solution, although not an optimal one, is to use a graduated decision balloting procedure. First, the issue is framed as clearly as possible. Then a vote is taken on that issue. If more than 50 percent but less than 60 percent of the congregation supports the ballot measure, then the congregation, as previously agreed, will continue to deliberate on the issue without implementation. If the measure receives a vote of at least 60 percent but less than 75 percent, the congregation implements the idea on a trial basis for an agreed-upon length of time. If a certain ballot measure garners more than 75 percent of the votes cast the congregation proceeds as if there is complete agreement.

Unanimity is rare. Waiting for total consensus is disaster, especially in a medium-sized or large congregation. Holding an unrealistic expectation of a vision without some dissenters will surely bring a crippling paralysis. Chapter nine deals in more detail about handling the inevitable conflict that choosing a vision brings.

A map of future action

The second stage of the plan phase is to actually construct a detailed map of specific actions. This map directs the changes necessary to move the congregation toward the newly chosen vision horizon. This is the part of the process everyone has eagerly awaited. Up to this point many have said, "Get on with it," and "When are we going to do something?" This is the stage where the congregation finally identifies and puts together what it will do. Hopefully, the leadership has resisted the impulse to do this earlier in the process, for this detailed map only has meaning as it arises out of a well-defined vision. Once the congregation chooses a vision that ignites maximum commitment within the body, the vision team can lead the congregation to add definition to the plan. Momentum is rising to a crescendo and more and more members are becoming involved. Word is spreading to the community that something exciting is happening at the church down the lane.

The key to all this is vision. It is the ingredient necessary to implement the turn around of a plateaued or declining congregation. God's inspired vision is the only way to motivate the body of Christ to rise up and cry out, "Let us start building!"

As the comprehensive plan to support the vision is put together, the congregation is ready to learn from the experience of other Christian bodies. Chapter seven details proven contemporary mission strategies for the membership to consider. Carefully and prayerfully, these strategies are considered and only those that directly move the vision forward are chosen.

Reflection questions

1. In addition to Nehemiah, what biblical examples of vision can you think of?

2. What is your personal mission in life? Reflect on how your own sense of vision interacts with the vision of the congregation.

3. How has your congregation done decision-making in the past? How can it be improved?

Notes

1. Stephen R. Covey, A. Roger Merrill, and Rebecca R. Merrill, *First Things First: To Live, To Love, To Learn, To Leave a Legacy* (New York: Simon & Schuster, 1994), 110.

2. Richard Gorsuch, (unpublished lecture, Fuller Theological Seminary, Pasadena, Calif., February 1997.)

3. Robert Logan and Thomas Clegg, *Releasing Your Church's Potential* (Carol Stream, Ill.: ChurchSmart Resources, 1998), p. 1.14.

4. Stephen R. Covey, *The Seven Habits of Highly Effective People: Restoring the Character Ethic* (New York: Simon & Schuster, 1989), 265.

7 Turning toward Health: Plan
Building Mission Strategies

Better use medicines at the outset than at the last moment.

Pubilius Syrus, maxim 866

Your long-put-off physical is now almost complete. With final instructions, your doctor scribbles on her prescription tablet some medication she believes you need to once again balance your health. Her choice of medication is not haphazard, however. It is based on her detailed analysis of your physical condition combined with her vast knowledge of applicable pharmaceuticals. Behind this choice lies years of research into the production of this particular drug, followed by exhaustive clinical trials on real patients. This data has been carefully reviewed by your physician before making this decision. Based on this accumulation of experience, this is the best option for what ails you.

Similar logic can be applied to congregations that have diagnosed their unique dysfunctions or uncovered their hidden weaknesses. However, research on cutting-edge mission strategies for the Christian church is not quite as systematic as research by pharmaceutical companies on promising new drugs. Still, we can learn from the experiences of other Christian churches. We can adapt their proven mission strategies to address areas of congregational ill health within each of our seven criteria for congregational health.

Throughout the Christian church in the United States and Canada, hard-won experience in innumerable congregations has demonstrated some specific mission strategies as having superior value to turn-around congregations. Witness the phenomenon of the past fifteen years in seminars and conferences for the continuing education of clergy and lay leaders. A shift has occurred away from the seminaries and other academies of learning in favor of seminars put on by innovative congregations or conferences featuring skilled congregational practitioners.

The ideas presented in this chapter may or may not be ones your congregation will choose to implement. The key, as has been argued throughout this book, is matching the mission strategy to the shared vision of the congregation. No single mission strategy is a cure-all for all congregations. This reality was demonstrated in the Church Membership Initiative of 1993 conducted among Lutheran churches in the United States. What this study found was that "growing congregations seem to have clergy and lay leadership working in a team, have a strong sense of being in mission that goes beyond their current membership, and provide a large number of different entry points to their congregations."[1] While this may not be terribly surprising, what did come as a bit of a surprise is that "congregations that are experiencing growth in ministry and membership utilize a wide variety of programs, resources, methods, and approaches to their mission."[2]

Let us take a look at each of the seven criteria and some representative examples of mission strategies with track records of restoring health. While not an exhaustive list, the following are offered in hopes of sparking your congregation into new modes of thinking in an effort to move it past its plateau.

Organization

Every modern corporation knows the reality of outdated bureaucracy. Shifting markets and changing paradigms force businesses large and small to realign their organizational structures. The very same phenomenon occurs in Christian churches, though congregations tend to be far less responsive. As Bob Dylan once sang "the times they are a-changin'." The mission field on which congregations are planted are a-changin' too.

However, too few congregations have reengineered their desperately outmoded organizational structures.

George Barna notes one such shifting reality on the domestic mission field. Barna has written that people in the United States are no longer interested in long-term commitments. He notes that "book clubs and record clubs no longer ask people to make long-term commitments—a marked change in the way they market their products."[3] The old practice of asking lay members to serve on committees for three-year terms is no longer successful. This emerging alteration in church volunteerism alone necessitates significant organizational changes in congregations.

Another example of factors that require organizational changes can be found in the attitudes of the baby boom generation (born between 1946 and 1964) and generation X (born between 1965 and 1979). These generations in particular are more interested in hands-on ministry than in attending one more meeting. Boomers and Xers have been in too many meetings that have inevitably devolved into lengthy ramblings or unproductive actions. These younger committee members then ask, "Who needs all these meetings?" and, more important, "Does it help anybody?" Barna's research suggests that short-term, hands-on duties with clear goals and expectations are what will motivate today's volunteers.

A congregation's newly chosen vision for mission forces a reexamination of the basic assumptions of its governance. Following its new vision, Trinity Church took a good long look at its organizational structure. What it found was shocking. Trinity's constitution and bylaws specified thirteen standing committees each requiring four to seven members. Thus, fifty-two to ninety-one members were needed just to manage the congregation's affairs. Worse still was the list of management duties delegated to these committee members, including attending monthly meetings with requisite reports and keeping current on pertinent information and activities involving the conference, synod, region, and national church. Each committee was to budget and allocate its funds (including more reports) along with performing long-range planning. With this much paperwork and meetings, how did ministry get done? The committed lay members of Trinity were mandated to spend so much time in meetings that they never got to the mission field!

Italian economist Vilfredo Pareto's study of elite social systems resulted in the now famous postulate that 20 percent of any group performs 80 percent of its work.[4] Applying this sociological phenomenon to Trinity then forces some basic mathematics. If Trinity has four-hundred confirmed members on the rolls and assuming that all are vital, active members (which is a more than generous assumption!) this twenty-eighty principle predicts that Trinity has eighty confirmed members who do 80 percent of the congregation's work. If the basic structure requires fifty-two to ninety-one members to fully operate, it begs the question: So who was left to actually carry out the ministry? If the eighty people who do 80 percent of the work are occupied with endless management duties, then the bulk of the congregation's potential has just been used up without ever directly touching human needs!

Larry Greiner in a 1972 article written for the *Harvard Business Review*[5] asserts that there are five identifiable developmental phases in the life of an organization that require revolution in order to continue growth. Figure 7.1 illustrates these periods of evolution and revolution. Greiner's work suggests that the church, like any other organization, must be able to revolutionize itself or it will not surmount the crisis. Congregations along with businesses "are likely to wither, fold, or to level off in their growth rates."[6]

One of the most important issues to negotiate is the changing role of the church governing board. King of Kings Lutheran Church, Shelby Township, Michigan, reorganized its governing structure around its mission and vision. The congregation designed three core teams—welcome, grow, and care. Each core team leader oversees the work of dozens of ministry teams—choirs, direct mail, parking lot greeters, community callers, worship guest follow-up, parent support, adult education, confirmation, Sunday school, telecare callers, health care, women's shelter support, blood drive servers, to name just a few. The

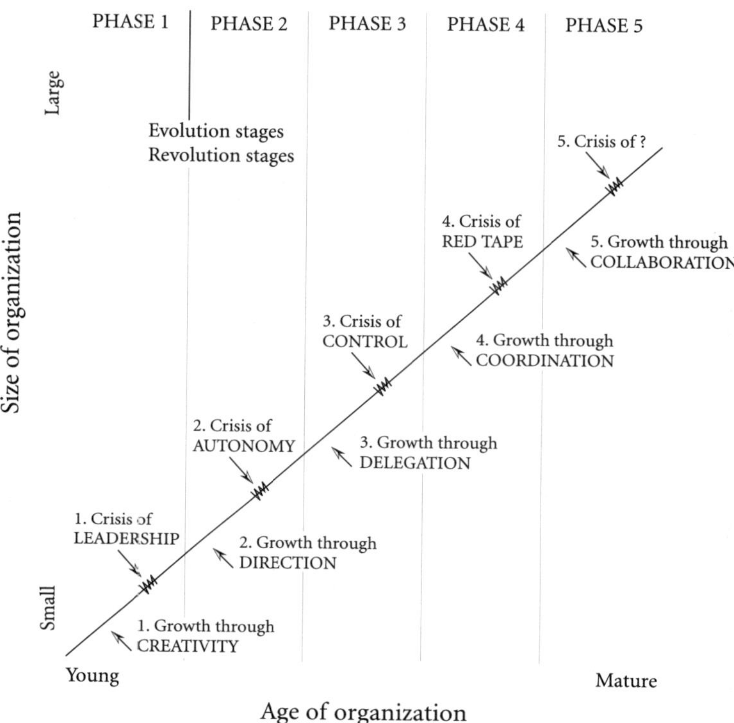

Fig. 7.1. Source: An exhibit from "Evolution and Revolution as Organizations Grow" by Larry Greiner, issue May–June 1998, *Harvard Business Review*. Exhibit copyright © 1998 by the President and Fellows of Harvard College. Reprinted by permission of *Harvard Business Review*.

congregation maintains a clear line between governance and ministry. The council provides strategic planning and makes sure the ministry teams have adequate financing, training, and leadership.[7]

Even as we consider the advantages of reorganization, a warning must be offered. Realigning a congregation's organizational structure more than once every decade will create the illusion of progress, while producing confusion, inefficiency, and demoralization.

Growth

We live in an age of rapid technological change. Computers, e-mail, voice mail, and other technologies, while freeing us from some elements of drudgery, also isolate people from each other. However, in the midst of this isolating change, witness the coffeehouse phenomenon. Little coffee shops are springing up everywhere around the country. These coffee shops are testimony to our need to make time to sit and talk with others in a more personal manner. We are searching for what *Cheers*, the 1980s television sitcom, promised: "a place where everyone knows your name."

Congregations of believers need to take this shifting reality of life in our society into account in order to grow as a congregation. To this end, small-group ministries have been instrumental in congregations around the country in meeting people's need for community, of being a place where everybody knows your name, not just your e-mail address!

St. Andrew Church was on the verge of closing. Membership had dwindled to only seventy and was rapidly declining. The congregation had poor leadership and was unable to pay its bills. However, because the surrounding community had so much potential, denominational leaders decided it was worth one more shot. Pastor Larry was called to begin work at St. Andrew. A new worship service that focused on celebration and praise drew the attention of visitors. In response to these new visitors, St. Andrew created "caring groups" to build community among and with them. Initially three small groups were formed. These groups quickly grew to fifteen and offered new people a place for spiritual growth and a community of other believers to share their journey of faith. Seven years later, St. Andrew has grown to almost four hundred members.

The example of St. Andrew illustrates an often overlooked facet of congregational life: Growth in a congregation will only occur if new points of entry into the social architecture of the membership are created. In a congregation with stable membership, the present social dynamics meet the needs of the existing members. These social dynamics have structure and may be seen as social architecture. Those new to the congregation find it difficult to break into these long-standing, natural social groupings. For this reason, strategies like adding worship services, initiating small-group ministries, and beginning other ministries are so effective in jump-starting new growth.

Small-group ministries are not a recent innovation. Small groups meeting for prayer and Bible study have been around since the days Jesus gathered his disciples. What is new in our time, however, is our craving for deeper relationships with other people because these human needs are not being met as readily elsewhere. Even given this need, small-group ministries are not easily formed. The congregation needs to thoroughly understand its unique subculture and then match its small-group strategy to the interests, gifts, and needs of that subculture. That is to say, how one does small-group ministry in a rural recreational setting, for example, will vary greatly from how it might be done in a fast-paced neighborhood of business executives. Whatever the subculture, the human needs remain the same. People need other people.

Invitational evangelism strategies such as door-to-door or telephone calling in the community or "bring-a-friend" Sundays are additional avenues for bringing people into community.

Movement

Enthusiasm is a precious commodity for a congregation that has experienced a lengthy downward spiral. Congregational inferiority complexes are easily born and hard to defeat. This makes it critical to give considerable attention to the matter of creating momentum. In the plan stage, the vision team will do well to craft a graduated strategy, beginning with actions that create enthusiasm, pride, and a feeling of success. The team should resist the temptation to begin all or even multiple actions simultaneously. The goal is not solely to take action but to foster a renewed spirit among the congregation.

Early actions are also chosen for their capacity to elicit attention from the surrounding community. A superior execution of initial plans will alter the community's negative perception of a congregation. A successful follow-up will then generate interest on the part of those neighbors who have long since dismissed the idea of attending the church.

Outreach to new residents, offering activities for children and families in the community, or English-as-a-second-language classes are all possibilities for forward movement that serve the community.

Transformation

One of the gravest dangers to any Christian congregation with a long history is institutionalization. The process of institutionalization is the pull on the organization to survive. The focal point becomes perpetuating the institution rather than the impulse to make disciples. Institutionalization is deadly to the spiritual mission of Christ's church. Older congregations must actively fight this inward decay by returning to their first love and asking for Christ's continual transformation.

If all has gone well to this point in the plan phase, then the congregation has rediscovered the power of corporate prayer. Prayer keeps us open to the new life God creates. Prayer is one of the central means God uses to transform us from the inside out. Rediscovering prayer as a central act of congregational life enhances the congregation's transformational ministry.

The vision team could consider taking prayer to a new level through the formation of prayer ministries. This is done by offering worship visitors the opportunity to pray with another believer before, during, or after worship. Instituting services for prayer and healing of the sick and distressed is another common avenue used by turn-around congregations to release prayer's transformative power.

Transformation by the power of the gospel is a process that is not solely intellectual but also experiential. Many successful turn-around congregations have enabled people to experience the grace of God through *Cursillo* (also known by other regional or denominational names such as *Walk to Emmaus* [United Methodist]; *Tres Diaz, Via de Christo* [Lutheran]; and *Alpha.*)

Cursillo is a Spanish word that means "short course." Cursillo is a three-day, lay-led retreat wherein the participants are immersed in the love of God through lecture, prayer, worship, and showerings of grace through the ministry of other believers. The ministry of Cursillo has been used by God to activate thousands of persons for whom faith is only an intellectual exercise. Through a retreat such as Cursillo believers can experience the power of God transforming their lives.

In a similar style but designed for people just beginning in the faith is Alpha. The Alpha movement is a relative newcomer to the ministry of the church. An Alpha course is a ten-week practical exploration of the Christian faith. It is designed primarily for those who are not churchgoers and those new to the faith. This shining ministry was born out of Holy Trinity Brompton (HTB), London, England, more than twenty years ago and has since swept the globe, with thousands of participants worldwide.

Alpha North America's Web site describes Alpha as "a flexible and practical model that works for any group of any size. Churches and Christian organizations of every background and denomination are discovering it to be a simple and effective way of presenting the gospel of Jesus Christ in a clear and non-threatening manner to people from all walks of life."[8]

Sensitivity

Simply listening, carefully listening, to the unchurched people who live in the community is a major outreach strategy in itself. However, many congregations have defined listening to the needs of their unchurched neighbors as "You become like us and you are welcome here." Others have feared that in listening carefully they might have to change themselves, and so they choose not listen at all. Plateaued and declining congregations that wish to turn around their downward spiral must relearn how to listen to their unchurched neighbors. The study phase has provided data on the cultural, ethnic, and age makeup of the community around the congregation. It's possible distinct generational or language differences between the community and the congregation have been uncovered.

Becoming more sensitive to the gifts and needs of unchurched people requires creativity and commitment on the part of the congregation. Creativity is necessary to learn the deep needs and perceptions of these neighbors. It will take commitment from members to want to understand what is going on in the hearts and minds of community residents.

The vision team begins by interviewing those members of the congregation who have joined in the past year. The team asks them what their perceptions of the church were before they came, finds out what brought them and what their deepest needs were and are, and invites them to share their current attitudes toward the congregation. What does it look like in their eyes? How can it be improved? What needs to be changed? What is the congregation doing well?

Another strategy is door-to-door calling. This is done by preparing in advance a few basic questions. Each person who answers the door should know that the caller is just interested in meeting the church's neighbors and learning more about how the congregation might help meet their needs. The caller takes only a few minutes of each person's time and then moves on.

A third strategy is to commission congregational leaders to conduct in-depth interviews with two or three unchurched people with whom they have regular contact. A uniform questionnaire is compiled for each leader and then the data is collected and collated. A brief written summary for each member of the congregation is prepared for review.

Willow Creek Community Church of South Barrington, Illinois, and Saddleback Valley Community Church of Mission Viejo, California, both used such information to construct a caricature of a typical man and woman in their respective communities. Willow Creek called their representations "Unchurched Harry and Mary" while Saddleback referred to "Saddleback Sam." These caricatures enabled each ministry within these leading congregations to readily keep their unchurched neighbors in mind when planning their individual ministries.

Adaptation

No one would question the fact that our culture offers an unbelievable array of choices. As the people of Christ, sent into the world to baptize and teach all that Christ has commanded us, we must adapt to this multiple-choice world. U.S. culture has become accustomed to the shopping mall, where one-stop shopping is expected.

Nowhere is this reality clearer than in the arena of worship. Disparities in musical tastes accompanied by different expectations by the various generations of members have made offering multiple styles of worship services advantageous for some plateaued or declining congregations. While mission starts and congregational restarts can enjoy the luxury of one shared style of ministry, this advantage may not be possible in an older congregation. A radical shift in worship style could effect wholesale mutiny by those who have supported the church for decades. On the other hand, working harder at the same style of worship that was offered during the declining years is sheer suicide. Multiple services in varying styles and music can make a significant contribution to a congregational turn around.

Many successful turn-around congregations have contextualized their worship services to speak to the hearts of their community. These congregations have listened prayerfully and carefully to the concerns of the community and have planned worship so these persons can experience God's love breaking into their hearts and transforming their minds in Christ Jesus. Some may offer an additional service that has music and an informal style to appeal to baby boomers, or perhaps they offer a Spanish-language service for the growing number of Spanish-speaking residents in the community.

This worship plan begins with a vision. Worship, no less than the rest of the congregation's ministry, needs to be supported by a shared vision. Is it the desire of the membership to offer worship services for seekers who are unsure of the truth claims of the gospel? Or is it more appropriate to bring folks into the depths of God's mystery and drama through the high liturgy of the church? Either strategy can be highly effective.

The key ingredient is a deeply shared vision that releases the congregation's greatest potential for singing the heart song of the community in glory and praise to God.

Reproduction

Left in the ocean for years without cleaning the hull, a ship will gather barnacles. In such condition the hull will be inefficient as it cuts through the seas. So too is the church after decades of ministry. The barnacles of good but nonessential programs begin to crowd out the intentional discipling of a new generation of believers.

We no longer live in a society dominated by the Christian church. As such, many mission strategies from the first two centuries after Christ are seeing resurgence. One such strategy is that of the catechumenate. In the early church, the catechumenate was a period of intense instruction into the Christian faith prior to baptism or membership. The Alpha course mentioned previously is one such example, as are the Roman Catholic Rite of Christian Initiation for Adults (RCIA) program, the rejuvenated catechumenate in the Lutheran church, or other extended new-member incorporation efforts.

A mission strategy that seeks to place renewed importance on active discipleship of youth as well as new believers is essential to the reproductive health of a congregation. The fact that most individuals become Christians before age eighteen compels every congregation to provide a strong youth ministry. Congregational size is of no significance. Every resource necessary must be expended for the establishment of a vital ministry to young people so that they can experience the living God.

Reproduction, in the congregational sense, also involves giving birth to a new generation of leaders. A common characteristic of plateaued and declining congregations is a lack of leadership development. In such congregations the training of leaders has been only on-the-job. Such implicit methods produce only a one-for-one replacement strategy. To turn a congregation from maintenance to vitality requires a leadership development program that multiplies leaders. One established leader mentors two or three or maybe even four new leaders, thus growing the congregation's leadership resources for outreach. A consistent, reproducible model for intentional development of new and better leaders is a proven strategy for restoring congregational health.

Strategies for action

The mission strategies detailed above are by no means an inclusive list, but rather a suggestion of what has been effective in other congregations. The bibliography on pages 130–132 and *Catching the Next Wave Workbook* identify sources of more in-depth assistance with mission strategies. In addition, leaders of other congregations in the community and denomination or judicatory personnel can offer insight and assistance. The important matter is to choose mission strategies to fit your newly discerned vision by addressing your congregation's health. The vision team helps the congregation to shape its strategies into a concrete plan.

Throughout the plan phase, congregational leadership, both lay and pastoral, will be tested to the limits. Strong Christian leadership is the key factor in the successful plan and that is the topic of chapter eight.

Reflection questions

1. Brainstorm a few mission strategies that fit your congregation's vision.

2. Where do you see or sense momentum? What will produce the maximum momentum in your congregation?

Notes

1. Alan C. Klaas and Cheryl D. Brown, *Church Membership Initiative: Narrative Summary of Findings and Research Summary of Findings* (Appleton, Wis.: Aid Association for Lutherans, 1993), 3.

2. Ibid.

3. George Barna, *The Frog In The Kettle: What Christians Need To Know About Life in the 21st Century* (Ventura, Calif.: Regal Books, 1990), 35.

4. Kennon L. Callahan, *Twelve Keys to an Effective Church* (San Francisco: Harper & Row, 1983), xviii.

5. Larry E. Greiner, "Evolution and Revolution As Organizations Grow," *Harvard Business Review* 50, no. 4 (July–August 1972): 37–46.

6. Ibid., 40.

7. Louis R. Forney, "Organizing to Be Mission Focused and Permission Giving," *The Discipling Congregation* (Summer 1998).

8. Information cited from Alpha North America's Web site, www.alphana.org.

8 Turning toward Health: Act
Leadership for Action

Vision without action is a daydream.
Action without vision is a nightmare.

Japanese proverb

Design. Study. Plan. Act. To some it seems like the congregation is wasting time with all this studying and planning. Others complain that things are moving along too fast. Neither of these viewpoints, if held by a minority of your membership, is an accurate gauge of the process to date. Rather, the prime evidence that your congregation is prepared to move into the act phase lies in the mood and temper of the majority of the general membership.

Congregational readiness

If all has gone gracefully, there will be a profound sense of trust, newly born, among the people. The congregation has garnered new skills and learned throughout the process itself how to live in community with one another. Honest dialogue about the issues facing the congregation has replaced the silent games being played. There will also be an increase in congregational energy and, alongside it, a corresponding increase in tension among the membership.

The vision has given birth to a broader ownership of the congregation's mission. More members are committed or enrolled in the shared vision and fewer are simply compliant with the will of the majority. The congregation now knows how to lead and how to be led. Followership is enhanced because people are committed to the plans they themselves helped to create. These are all issues of communal trust. This is the spark the congregation needs before it acts.

Another critical indicator that the congregation is prepared to move to action is an increasing hopefulness about the future of the congregation. Hope is born anew due to escalating enthusiasm. The congregation at large is feeling better about its future. Pessimism is dying and the old congregational cycle of failure and inferiority is fading away. Hopefulness is seen on the part of the larger community as well as within the rolls of the congregational membership. It is time to catch the wave of action when both the congregation and the community now believe that their hope for a renewed mission is achievable.

The emergence of new leaders is a further indicator of readiness for action. The process to date has helped to identify those with leadership gifts. Renewed hope infuses these persons with the motivation to step forward into positions of greater responsibility. They detect the stirring of the Holy Spirit in their hearts as a call to service and action. These persons can be mentored into multiplying more leaders for the renewed mission. No longer are the same people being asked to lead but new folks are stepping forth to serve.

The vision team is now ready to complete its work and hand back the reins to the selected or elected officials of the congregation. Its goals have been met; its task complete. Now it is time for the regular organizational machinery of the congregation to implement the plan that has been structured with a well-thought-out timeline graduated to maximize momentum. It is the responsibility of the church governing body to initiate the individual action steps for a rejuvenated mission.

Action planning

Each of these calculated, individual actions are miniature versions of the process the entire congregation has undergone. For example, if the first action decided upon was to establish a vibrant youth ministry, then the congregation will already understand how to form a youth vision task force as a first action. This team leads those involved in the youth ministry through the phases of design, study, plan, act, and tend in the very same manner as the entire congregation experienced. These phases proceed much faster since the process is now a familiar one and much of the research is, no doubt, already in hand.

The method of using temporary task forces is the same as with the vision team. The leadership body of the congregation commissions task forces to midwife the designated mission strategies from birth into life. The governing body entrusts the task forces with two or, at most, three very specific goals. From the outset these goals allow the task forces to focus on their singular task. They also enable the teams to know when they have completed their work. This instills a sense of fulfillment in accomplishing their task.

Just as before, chair positions are carefully chosen from among the most respected and trusted leaders among the members. This is especially important for the first few actions to be implemented. The trust-building process is still going on in the congregation. Having well-known and respected leaders chair the first several task forces will solidify the congregation's trust in this process. Later actions can then use an emerging leader without fear that the congregation will not trust this task force. Each chair needs to have the gifts that fit the task assigned by the governing body. After the person has consented to lead, members are chosen with a broad representation of various constituencies. A mix of member giftedness is essential to success.

The newly created task forces report back to the governing body and, especially, communicate frequently with the congregation, keeping it fully informed of their labors. The task forces follow the same process: design, study, plan, act, and tend. Their goal is to involve as many willing members as possible to create a vision for the planned mission strategy, followed by a cohesive plan to be implemented.

When the task forces determine the appropriate moment has come for action, they disband and turn over the final two phases of act and tend to a duly authorized governing body of the congregation. The task forces' last duty before disbanding is to produce a final, written report. This report is essential to promote long-term continuity with leaders who will follow in the years to come.

Although action is being taken on the carefully designed plan and the work of the vision team is over, the turn-around process is far from complete. Within this present act phase, two matters require thoughtful handling. The first is the matter of leadership development and support and the second is that of management of the conflict that will inevitably arise from leading people in new directions.

Leadership skills

Without gifted leadership the congregation never arrives at this act phase. Leadership is the critical ingredient to consummating the turn around through appropriate action. To this end, it behooves the congregation's governing body to examine the congregation's leadership development program. The remainder of this chapter focuses on the particular leadership skills necessary for the successful actions leading to a turn around.

A congregational turn around simply does not happen without a strong combination of lay and pastoral leadership. Lay leadership is often undervalued. No pastor or church staff is ever able to pull the sled all by themselves. Nor should they! The apostle Paul's metaphor for the church, the body of Christ, reminds us that we all must share our gifts for the body to be healthy and whole. No one person is indispensable nor is any one person unnecessary.

Pastoral leadership must also be present for the congregation to ever have the opportunity to reverse its death thrall. George Barna, in *Turnaround Churches*, even goes so far as to suggest that what the congregation needs is a "strong leader from the outside to accomplish the turnaround." Barna quotes Pastor Richard Germain: "The leader is the key. I used to fight that contention. . . . But I have come to realize that if the pastor blocks this, if the pastor is indifferent to growth, if he [or she] doesn't have vision, if he [or she] just wants to go along, not much is going to happen."[1]

Thinking outside the box

Among the most important skills for congregational leaders to acquire is the mental skill of thinking in new paradigms. All human beings have the tendency to unconsciously hold fast to particular ways of viewing the world. It is painfully difficult to break through these old paradigms and to see matters from an alternate perspective. Albert Einstein captured this need when he said the significant problems we face cannot be solved at the same level of thinking we were at when we created them.[2] Einstein's maxim is doubly true in plateaued or declining congregations led by members of long-standing involvement.

Leaders can acquire new paradigms in several ways. They can attend any number of excellent seminars across the country that challenge them to think in new ways about their mission. Another method is to assume the perspective of a completely unchurched person with zero knowledge of the Christian faith. The opposite approach can also work—adopting the viewpoint of a neighbor who has lived next to the church all his life, thinks he knows everything about the faith, and wants no part of it. By reading Scripture as part of a daily devotional routine and studying Bible texts with other congregational members, people and ways of thinking are changed. What is learned by thinking "outside the box"? Undoubtedly, such mental exercises lift congregational leadership to new levels of awareness that can lead to solving the problems of the congregation.

Strategic planning

Leaders can learn valuable skills from championship chess players. Championship chess is played five, ten, even fifteen moves ahead of the actual positions of the chess pieces. Each player analyzes possible moves and counter moves so as to look down the road for the best way to victory. So it is with effective congregational leadership. Leaders are most effective when they think into the future like a chess master.

Such strategic thinking is dynamic rather than static. A leader who has a set agenda comes across as simply selling. Such is the wisdom captured in the familiar proverb: The leader who gets too far in front of his people is often mistaken for the enemy. Instead, the strategic congregational leader has mentally mapped out a critical path forward, all of which changes immediately in response to the dynamic events occurring in the congregation.

Business leaders or project engineers are excellent resource people for teaching strategic skills such as this. They will be likely candidates to introduce sophisticated planning tools from the business world such as Gantt charts and PERT (Program Evaluation and Review Technique) diagrams.[3] Gantt charts (see figure 8.1) were first devised by engineer Henry Gantt in the early 1900s. His method uses a horizontal bar chart to demonstrate the relationship between individual steps in a complex project. PERT diagrams (see figure 8.2) are more sophisticated and are appropriate for projects with many interactive steps. In a PERT diagram events are represented by a circle (or other shapes) and activities are arrows connecting these events. Dotted lines connect events between which no work is required. PERT diagrams are most useful if they show the time scheduled for completing an activity on the activity line.

Gantt chart

Fig. 8.1

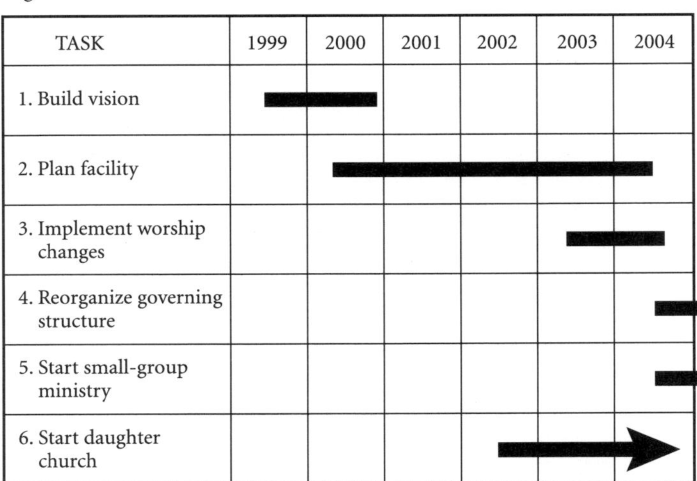

TASK
1999
2000
2001
2002
2003
2004
1. Build vision
2. Plan facility
3. Implement worship changes
4. Reorganize governing structure
5. Start small-group ministry
6. Start daughter church

Time (in years)

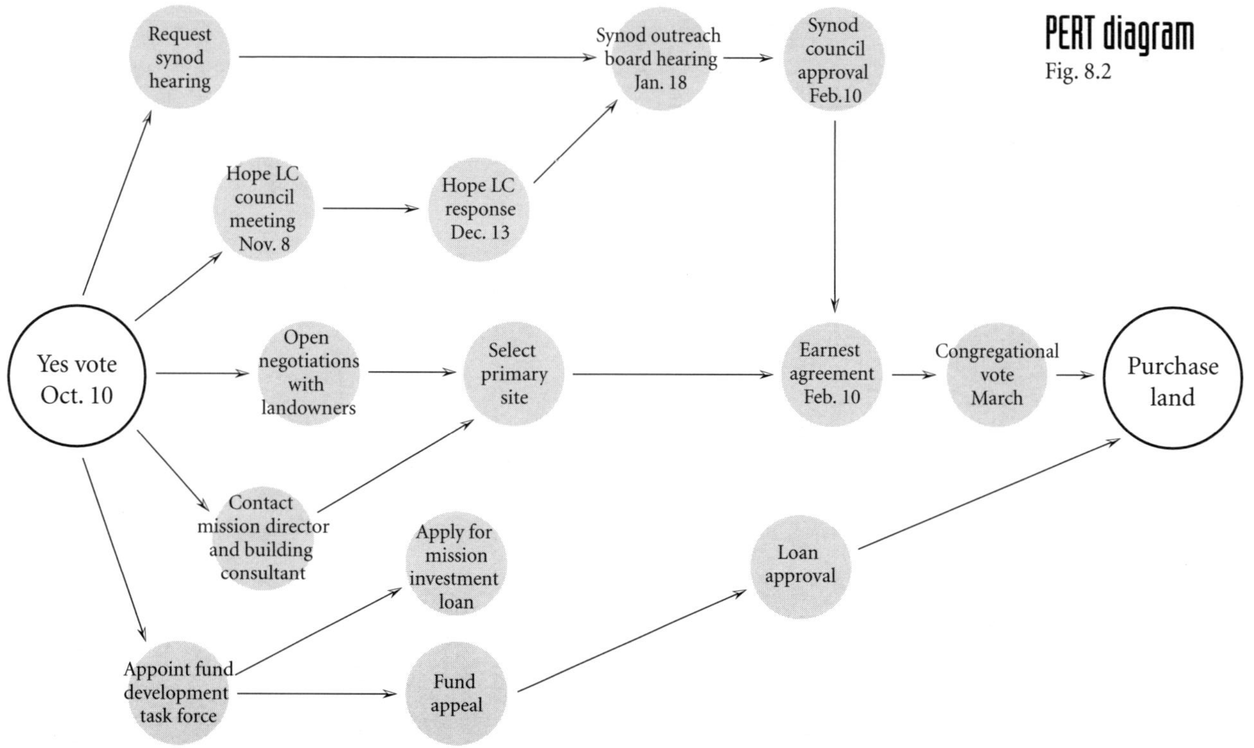

PERT diagram
Fig. 8.2

Leadership that uses this type of strategic thinking is more likely to project to the membership a nonanxious presence. By carefully thinking through the strategy for the process in advance and remaining fluid in reacting to the congregation, the leader is able to lower the general anxiety in the body as a whole. Followers are less stressed when they have confident leaders. Stress is further reduced when members are able to graphically see the steps required to achieve their goals through diagrams such as Gantt or PERT charts.

Choosing battles

Another technique that can be gleaned from chess masters is the expertise of knowing when to sacrifice a piece. In other words, an important skill in congregational leadership lies in knowing which battles to lose in order to win the war. Not every battle is worth fighting. It is a matter of wise discernment to know when to back down and relent even when you believe you are right. Leaders who are flexible and willing to compromise, and are perceived as such, are more effective at serving in the long run.

On the other hand, wise leaders know which issues are essential. Limited resources must be spent in those areas that will have the maximum impact toward restored health.

Systems thinking

A third thinking-skill requisite for congregational leadership is what Peter Senge calls "system thinking." Senge explains: "Business and other human endeavors are also systems. They, too, are bound by invisible fabrics of interrelated actions, which often take years to fully play out their effects on each other. Since we are part of that lacework ourselves, it's doubly hard to see the whole pattern of change. Instead, we tend to focus on snapshots of isolated parts of the system, and wonder why our deepest problems never get solved. Systems thinking is a conceptual framework, a body of knowledge and tools that has been developed over the past fifty years, to make the full patterns clearer, and to help us see how to change them effectively."[4]

Leaders of plateaued or declining congregations need to stretch into thinking about these "interrelated actions" on several levels at the same time. There is first the action itself—a member said something unkind to another member in the heat of a meeting—which causes a conflict in itself. On a larger level, what was said may reflect a conflict between two competing constituencies that exhibit poor communication with one another. Stretching even further, this seemingly localized exchange of heated words may have implications that affect the perceptions of their respective groups as well as those outside the congregation in the community at large. A successful intervention must use systems thinking to bring about the fullest measure of healing not only to the original feuding members but also to indirect participants in the larger systems of the congregation.

Local social workers or family therapists would be especially fruitful resources for raising awareness of these human systems. One strategy is to invite such skilled people to share their gifts in the congregation's leadership training program. The work of Virginia Satir, Murray Bowen, or Edwin Friedman may be particularly helpful.

Focusing like a laser beam

Lasers are no longer a thing of science fiction but a daily reality—we use laser pointers at meetings and lasers drive our CD-ROMs. The word *laser* is technically an acronym for *l*ight *a*mplified by *s*timulated *e*mission of *r*adiation. A laser is, quite simply, focused radiation. The laser provides an apt metaphor for congregational leadership. Focus is critical to accomplish the turn around so prayerfully desired. Too little focus and all is for naught.

A plateaued or declining congregation has so many needs it is hard for one to know where to begin rebuilding. It is altogether too tempting for congregational leaders to begin in the area most in need of improvement or in a ministry especially near and dear to their hearts. This is an often-repeated mistake. Remember: Shoot the biggest bear in camp first! Congregational leaders must build a shared vision first and then strategically plan to focus vital energy in well-chosen areas that support the vision. Then, and this is the hard part, leaders must let the rest go as is! Such focus enables the congregation to specialize in a few areas, developing excellence that distinguishes it from others in the community. Other local congregations can be strong in their areas of giftedness, creating a cohesive and coordinated body of Christ in the broader context, as God so earnestly desires.

Bringing the lumber

In a process as complex as the turn around of a plateaued or declining congregation, it is the responsibility of leaders "to bring the lumber." In other words, congregational leaders are called upon to assemble the raw materials: resources, scenarios, and research that the membership needs to make its wisest decisions. Census data, specialized books, outside consultants, and resources from denominational bodies are all components that, when put together in a creative process, enhance the outcome and expedite the process.

Once these raw materials are gleaned, the congregation is able to build as the Holy Spirit directs. Once the "lumber" is delivered, the leadership must be willing to share in the final shaping of what is created. It is a matter of trust that the Holy Spirit will work in mysterious ways to animate the body of Christ to accomplish Christ's will. If leaders are too directive in how resources are put to use, members will react negatively, perceiving that there is a hidden agenda lurking among the leadership. A negative perception like this may gradually bring all the hard work to ruin.

Doing the homework

Perhaps all of us can close our eyes and still hear our parents feverishly admonishing us to do our homework! It was good advice then and is good advice now. Inherent in turn arounds is the responsibility of the leadership to do its homework carefully. Just as we were all taught in school, doing our homework pays off in unexpected achievements. So too in the congregation.

Doing our homework means that leaders have assisted the congregation by carefully preparing, collating, and summarizing. Like a good administrative assistant to an effective executive, leaders facilitate congregational decision making by their hard work. Leaders pull their own weight and use their gifts to the glory of God. Leaders who do their homework with excellence inspire their followers to similar heights.

For the harvest

The very thought of becoming a leader in a social system that is stagnant or even malignant will frighten the most hardened, capable leaders. Questioning cultural assumptions and initiating reform, even in the least toxic of congregational circumstance, will bring about dreaded conflict and perhaps even painful social ostracism (see the next chapter on overcoming obstacles). This reality will force the congregation to intentionally develop a plan to promote and support leaders.

Still, even with the most elaborate and efficient leadership development program, conflict in a turn-around congregation is inevitable. No leadership development plan is complete without preparing those same leaders for the normal experience of the clash of ideas and power structures that accompanies change. Isaac Newton's observation about physical bodies is true also of the actions the congregation plans to undertake: Every action has an equal and opposite reaction.

Reflection questions

1. How does your congregation mentor and train the leaders it needs for its current organization?

2. Who among your members has the gifts to help train new congregational leaders in the skills needed for a turn around?

3. Is your congregation fervently following Jesus' directive: "Ask the Lord of the harvest to send out laborers into his harvest" (Matthew 9:38)?

Notes

1. Barna, *Turnaround Churches*, 72.

2. Covey, *Seven Habits of Highly Effective People*, 42.

3. Marion E. Haynes, *Project Management,* rev. ed., (Los Altos, Calif.: Crisp Publications, 1996), 30–39.

4. Senge, *Fifth Discipline*, 7.

9 Turning toward Health: Act
Overcoming Obstacles

For where God built a church, there
the Devil would also build a chapel.

Martin Luther
Table Talk

Grace Church was on a ten-year decline in worship attendance following a major congregational split that resulted in a significant exodus of members. The painful congregational conflict that preceded the split taught the remaining members to fear conflict and avoid it at all costs. As a result, even as the congregation quite obviously declined, the membership could not face up to its predicament. Conflict was increasingly feared because it replayed the group's collective memories of the dramatic upheaval of the body years before.

However, by the power of God, Grace Church experienced a turn around that was initiated by a committed lay person. Through this single member's able leadership the members began to see a need to step forward in faith. A vibrant youth ministry was born, drawing young families to the congregation once again. A few years later an energetic pastor was called to lead the congregation to determine its vision for mission. Growth began to accelerate as the community perceived the transformed nature of this long-standing church.

At this point, one might be tempted to think that all was right with Grace Church. However, the addition of the youth ministry combined with the renewed growth of the congregation set off a very painful series of congregational conflicts. These conflicts were destroying both lay and pastoral leadership. The situation was especially directed toward the pastor who endured very personal attacks on his character and the collateral effects on his wife and children. Consequently, the congregation was dangerously close to repeating its history of exploding into fragments and the resulting skid toward death of this body.

Conflict is not simply a reality for the plateaued or declining congregation but for the turn-around congregation as well. An individual who has cancer has a disease that causes him or her pain. Surgery to remove the cancer, while effecting a cure, is invasive and elicits more pain before the desired healing can take place. So, too, with turn-around congregations. Intervention through leadership strategies is not a universal salve preventing any more conflict. Rather, the turn-around process surfaces the hidden conflicts that already exist and creates even more. Given this fact, a book on leadership strategies for turn-around congregations would be incomplete without dealing with the subject of conflict.

This chapter develops an understanding of conflict, helps congregational leadership to prepare for conflict, and suggests strategies to transform conflict into forward momentum for the congregation.

Understanding conflict

Why did conflict erupt at Grace Church once the turn around was under way? The work of the late Edwin Friedman is of enormous help in finding an explanation for the turmoil at Grace. Friedman was an ordained Jewish rabbi and a practicing family therapist who molded both of his educational backgrounds into a revolutionary approach for understanding the processes within synagogues and churches. Applying an idea first derived from family systems theory, which is a prevalent model used by psychotherapists, Friedman suggests that congregations develop what psychologists call *homeostasis*. Homeostasis is "the tendency of any set of relationships to strive perpetually, in self-corrective ways, to preserve the organizing principles of its existence."[1]

Friedman's insight into homeostasis helps us understand why conflict intensified once Grace Church began to grow again. In its decade-long decline, a new homeostasis had been formed. Members shared a common, though unspoken, identity as the faithful remnant of believers left after the split. They subconsciously believed they were smaller now because they alone were holding fast to the historic faith while other neighboring churches were sacrificing the gospel and becoming captive to the culture. In actuality, members were blind to the fact that smaller was more comfortable for them. They did not have to adapt to new people nor was change necessary.

The turn around upset this homeostasis, throwing the congregational system into imbalance. The imbalance created tension that erupted into both open and submerged conflict. The cycle of congregational implosion was on the verge of repeating itself.

Conflict within Christian congregations seems especially dangerous. Perhaps it is because the Scriptures set such a high ideal for communities of Christians. Or maybe it is because Paul speaks so much in his letters about mutual fellowship and consolation. In any case, modern Christians often harbor the mistaken notion that a true Christian community is free of conflict. This is not just a benign myth but can actually make conflicts within Christian communities much worse than they need to be. The powerful myth that conflicts don't happen between Christians forces problems below the surface where they are harder to treat and where healing becomes more difficult.

Just what is a conflict? H. Newton Malony, senior professor of psychology at Fuller Theological Seminary's School of Psychology, defines conflict as "desperate feelings of threats to one's self-esteem that can lead to drastic acts of self-defense."[2] Granted, Malony offers a unique definition of conflict. Conflict is commonly viewed as something external to us. We see conflict as the striking together of two parties in opposition to each other and thus see the issue as the real conflict. Instead, Malony's insightful way of understanding conflict is to locate conflict inside an individual. From Malony's point of view, problems, as opposed to conflicts, are "differences of opinion about ways, means, or ends."[3]

Typically, people see the problem as the conflict. Rather, Malony forces us to see that our reactions to the problems put ourselves into conflict. Conflict is inside of us because we feel threatened and react defensively. This defensive reaction, or in some cases offensive reaction, is what inflames the conflict even further. Here is where our misunderstanding lies, due in large measure to the self-centered blinders we all wear. "It is not my fault," we protest to ourselves and to the world, "you are to blame." By locating conflict more accurately inside our own hearts we can begin to acquire a more healthy perspective on this universal experience of life.

Author and professor of psychology David Augsburger argues that conflict is "normal, natural, neutral, narrow, and mutual."[4] Conflict is first of all *normal.* Christians especially must release their widely held belief that conflict is abnormal and therefore to be avoided at all costs. Conflict is normal in that it adheres to a regular pattern of human experience. When humans live in relationship to one another, it is normal for them to experience conflict. That is to say, conflict is not necessarily an indicator that there is anything pathological or toxic in, among, or between conflicted parties.

Conflict is also *natural.* Here Christians can find the witness of Scripture to be supportive. The epistle to the Ephesians instructs us that "we were by nature children of wrath, like everyone else" (Ephesians 2:3). The theological doctrine of sin informs us that we have inherited sin from our first parents, Adam and Eve, and that we cannot escape this condition. Ephesians goes on to tell us of the only remedy, "For by grace you have been saved through faith, and this is not your own doing; it is the gift of God—not the result of works, so that no one may boast" (Ephesians 2:8-9). The truth is that we all are, as Martin Luther put it, simultaneously sinners and saints. Conflict is natural to us because of our self-centered ways of wishing the world, and everyone in it, revolved around us.

Conflict is *neutral,* which is to say that conflict is inherently neither good nor bad. We mistake what conflict is when we automatically conclude that conflict is bad and thus to be averted. This inaccurate perception often inflames conflict through avoidance or through too strong a defense, each of which makes matters worse than they need to be.

Conflict is *narrow*. In order for conflict to have any hope of resolution it must be narrowly and precisely defined. Too often conflict rages out of control because a minor problem, as Malony would define it, soon becomes about everything else one is feeling.

Conflict is *mutual*. Even though we have defined conflict as existing within an individual, conflict is mutual to at least two parties. This mutuality necessitates communication between parties that share the same conflict in order to reach a solution. Honest assessment of what is conflicted inside of us combined with skillful communication with the other parties in the problem enables the reduction of the internal conflict.

Educating the congregation about what conflict is and dispelling the common myths about conflict not only benefits the congregation as a whole but also each individual. A significant portion of the general angst felt by the congregation at the very presence of conflict is reduced. With a proper understanding of conflict in hand members can use conflict to their benefit, transforming this energy into forward momentum toward their Christ-given vision for mission.

Few people have had formal instruction in conflict. Just as few understand their own reactions to the conflict they experience internally. A congregation that seeks to turn around must take the issue of conflict with deadly seriousness. Initiating a turn around requires the leadership of the congregation to transform the normal, natural, neutral, and mutual conflict that predictably will occur.

For the individual, understanding conflict begins where conflict occurs: within ourselves. It is of enormous benefit to each leader to come to greater understanding of his or her own conflict resolution styles. Each of us has a preferred way of handling life's conflicts but our styles vary according to circumstance and the other parties involved. Our internal conflicts are often made more painful when we clash with others whose styles are opposite our own.

Upsetting a congregation's homeostasis erupts into painful conflict. This conflict frequently turns into quite personal attacks against the leaders of the threat to the status quo. Leaders who are unprepared for this may suffer disillusionment, despair, and even discouragement with the Christian church or, worse still, the Christian faith. The hoped-for congregational turn around is simply not possible without strong and faithful leaders who possess a healthy sense of who they are and who undertake these changes for Christ's sake.

Numerous passages of Scripture could be called upon to assist congregational leaders in seeing the need to be fully aware of the obstacles that lie ahead. The First Letter of Peter exhorts: "Discipline yourselves, keep alert. Like a roaring lion your adversary the devil prowls around, looking for someone to devour" (1 Peter 5:8). Growing in one's understanding of, and reactions to, conflict not only prepares strong congregational leaders but benefits the personal lives of the leaders as well.

Preparing for conflict

On the macroscopic level of the larger whole of the congregation, leaders must also be prepared for inescapable conflict. Conflict comes in many forms. However, there are several congregational conflicts that are more prevalent among turn arounds. Factions, rumor, and difficult people are the most vitriolic obstacles a turn-around church must overcome.

Factions

During the design phase the elected leadership first identified the varying constituencies of the congregation. These constituencies were distinguishable by their subtle dreams and fears for the congregation as well as by their shared values and beliefs with respect to the larger whole of the membership. These constituencies are put to use for the identification of a Christ-given, shared vision for mission.

Sometimes, however, these same constituencies, if they perceive the congregational changes as a threat to their values and beliefs, can become destructive factions working against other constituencies or the leadership. The phenomenon of congregational factions was one the apostle Paul knew all too well. Paul wrote this admonishment to the church at Corinth: "Now I appeal to you, brothers and sisters, by the name of our Lord Jesus Christ, that all of you be in agreement and that there be no divisions among you, but that you be united in the same mind and the same purpose. For it has been reported to me by Chloe's people that there are quarrels among you, my brothers and sisters" (1 Corinthians 1:10-11). The members of the Corinthian church had divided themselves into competing factions.

The danger of factions at war with each other was also not lost on the apostle. In his letter to the Galatians Paul writes: "Now the works of the flesh are obvious: fornication, impurity, licentiousness, idolatry, sorcery, enmities, strife, jealousy, anger, quarrels, dissensions, factions, envy, drunkenness, carousing, and things like these. I am warning you, as I warned you before: those who do such things will not inherit the kingdom of God" (Galatians 5:19-21). Note that Paul lists enmities, strife, dissensions, and factions with things he considered heinous evils—fornication, sorcery, drunkenness, and carousing. Factions are a serious threat to the health of a church.

Factions grow when there is little direct communication between constituencies. Healing occurs when members of each constituency sit and listen to one another. While it is still possible for opposing groups to be locked into what church conflict expert Speed Leas calls "intractable conflict,"[5] most factions can be dispersed simply by prayerful and careful listening to their sisters and brothers in Christ. As the apostle Paul appealed to the Corinthian factions to "be united in the same mind and the same purpose," a similar concentration prepares opposing factions to focus on the needs of the kingdom of Christ.

Rumor

A second destructive obstacle to the turn around of a plateaued or declining congregation is that of rumor. Rumors are formidable forces allied against the new changes taking place. It is of enormous benefit to congregational leadership to anticipate this problem and have an advance strategy for combating such negativity.

Rumor is an expected companion to a congregational turn around. It is natural to assume that the generation of rumors, working against the forward momentum of the congregation, is an intentional strategy of those opposed to the change. The research on rumors conducted during the World War II suggests otherwise. Understanding the process of rumor initiation and formation can assist turn-around leaders greatly.

As teachers at Harvard University in the 1940s, Gordon W. Allport and Leo Postman produced their classic volume on understanding the nature of rumors. Their work, *The Psychology of Rumor*,[6] offers superior research acquired during the tumultuous days of World War II when rumors abounded and threatened troops, military strategy, and the outcome of the war itself. Posters distributed by the Office of War Information reminded citizens that "Loose lips sink ships" or that "Enemy ears are listening." This time period provided Allport and Postman an excellent research climate.

Rumor is defined by Allport and Postman as "a specific (or topical) proposition for belief, passed along from person to person, usually by word of mouth, without secure standards of evidence being present."[7] Such propositions for belief serve to satisfy important emotional goals in a society or closed group such as a congregation. This is especially true at times of general crisis like that of a congregation shifting to a new pattern of ministry.

Rumors are a natural result of human beings' insatiable hunger for information. Rumor serves us by making the situation at hand simpler than it is in reality. Allport and Postman call this "effort after meaning."[8] This effort to find meaning is not inherently malicious but is fed by closed systems and systems that are not trusted. This is precisely what makes congregations with plateaued or declining membership particularly vulnerable to rumors.

The basic formula for the generation of rumor can be expressed simply: *R*umor = *I*ntensity × *A*mbiguity (R = I × A); that is to say, the quantity of rumor equals the intensity of the situation multiplied times the ambiguity of the information available. "Rumor travels when events have importance in the lives of individuals and when the news received about them is either lacking or subjectively ambiguous."[9]

If information that people want to know is not available, they are likely to spontaneously produce it. This should not be interpreted as deliberately planting false rumors. It is more accurate to say that when excitement of a particular group is high, rumors are generated spontaneously. In those very rare instances where a rumor is deliberated planted, those rumors that will be accepted by the group as valid are ones that align closely with what the group expects or desires. In such cases, these rumors are extremely difficult to eradicate even when proven false. This is due to the fact that these false rumors continue to support the believer's personal assumptions about what must be true.

The sad reality of rumors is that rumors abound seemingly endlessly! This is especially so when excitement is very high. In such circumstances, only the number of channels available limits the quantity of rumors. In other words, the maximum number of rumors is the number of possible relationships inside the group!

Allport and Gordon suggest three rules of rumor formation: leveling, sharpening, and assimilation. Rumors level information; in other words, rumors take information and make it repeatable by condensing the content. The once detailed information, when it becomes a rumor, is more concise and, as a consequence, is more understandable. In this manner, the information passes more readily from the person repeating the rumor to the recipient.

Information in rumors in sharpened. Hearers of rumors hear what they want to hear. Only those portions of the information that interest the hearer are retained. This sharpens those juicy parts of the story whereas, in the context of the complete set of information, these details would have less dramatic effect.

Recipients assimilate information passed on through hearsay into what they already believe or assume. Rumors become more consistent with such preexisting beliefs as elements from one's own existing set of expectations, fears, or desires are added. This has the effect of making the rumor more plausible to the hearer and more readily able to be believed. Information that evokes a high degree of emotion tends to distort this process. The original information, as it finds its way into rumor and is passed from ear to ear, becomes more and more contorted to fit each person's emotionally clouded preexisting beliefs, fears, and desires.

With a better understanding of rumors, the leadership of the congregation is better able to combat their ill effects on the forward progress of the body. The difficulty is attempting to diminish rumor in an emotionally charged environment. Common sense is to combat rumors by attacking them directly. This is actually counterproductive. Preaching and teaching against rumor will create more rumors!

Here the force field theory of researcher Kurt Lewin is most instructive. Lewin, in his book *Resolving Social Conflicts*,[10] describes any problem situation as a balance between "driving forces" and "restraining forces." Driving forces, in the case of rumor, are those forces existing within individuals that compel them to search for meaning in the present circumstances or with the issue in question. Restraining forces are those efforts at restricting or opposing the driving force producing the rumor.

With this operating concept, Lewin argues that the solution is not to increase the restraining forces—in this case, directly fighting the rumor to attempt to prove it false. This method only serves to increase the driving forces, because folks conclude "they must have something to hide" or "there must be more to this after all, given all the energy they are putting into fighting it."

Instead, the solution to eradicating rumor is to work toward decreasing the driving forces that produce the rumors in the first place. When information is readily available to members before they begin to exert effort to discover it for themselves, the drive toward rumor is decreased. When the environment is less emotionally charged through efforts at alleviating members' anxiety and grief, then the spontaneous production of rumors is minimized.

Difficult people

Every Christian congregation has difficult people within its ranks. Generally speaking, in a healthy congregational system these folks, though still expressing their unique quirks and oddities, pose little threat to the life and health of the body. The situation is quite different in the case of a declining congregation. In the downward cycle of the congregation, these difficult people generally are not the ones who leave. As the system shrinks, these people, who once functioned satisfactorily in the larger congregational body, now accumulate power in a smaller church system.

When the congregation comes to a new plateau at a much smaller size, these very same difficult people now are a much greater threat to the health of the congregation. It is as if the system has distilled itself into a very unhealthy collection of believers. Understanding how to deal with these unhealthy people is an absolute necessity if a turn around is ever to occur.

Several considerations aid immensely in dealing with difficult people. First, difficult people should be given as little attention and energy as is possible to deal with problem at hand. The more attention given to problem members, the more power is handed to them. The temptation to drop everything to put out the fire must be resisted. Rather, with a little humility and much good humor, leaders should listen carefully to what "problem" members have to say and press ahead as Christ so leads.

Second, Kenneth Haugk, founder of Stephen Ministries and author of *Antagonists in the Church*, advises leaders against using public means of communication to deal with antagonists.[11] Doing so only increases the restraining forces on the antagonist and makes matters more difficult. Furthermore, it undermines the positive forces among members who are unaware of the problem.

Third, difficult people within a Christian congregation should be dealt with courageously in an open, direct manner wrought out of biblical and theological integrity. It is altogether too easy to avoid conflict with a difficult member. This is neither healthy nor faithful. Christ calls us to model healthy communication that seeks the best interests of the individual balanced with the best interests of the entire body.

The fourth tactic in dealing with difficult people is to maintain an unwavering focus on the vision for mission that Christ has given to the body. This eases the pain members feel when a difficult person, who has been loved despite the wounds they have inflicted upon the congregation, decides to relinquish his or her membership. Such believers are rarely lost to the kingdom but only transferred to another part of the body of Christ.

Finally, leaders can continue to prayerfully commit difficult people to Christ. Prayer serves to remind us that all of us are, in one way or another, difficult people in God's eyes. That is the very nature of sin. Prayer bequeaths us a measure of humility, along with a dose of courage, mixed with compassion. Prayer further reminds us that we are not the messiah. Jesus is Lord of the church and he alone is Savior.

The reality of evil

In the words that open this chapter, Martin Luther intended more than firing off another of his famous one-liners. Luther understood the power of evil, which seeks to undermine the kingdom of God. While we do not want to go around searching for devils behind every bush, as was the mind-set in the late Middle Ages, neither do we want to blithely ignore this supernatural reality.

Transforming conflict

In the pictorial alphabet of the Chinese people, the word for crisis is a combination of the symbols for danger and opportunity. This bit of ancient wisdom, it would seem, also applies to conflict in the congregation. Conflict in a Christian congregation poses a danger, which we can clearly see, but also presents an opportunity for growth.

Conflict, as it exists inside the heart and soul of an individual and then is acted out in social behavior, first produces confusion. If this confusion can be directed into challenging one's own presupposition, then profound learning can take place. It is a wise student who can embrace such confusion, knowing that through it new ways of understanding the world are born.

Conflict produces energy. Harnessing this energy by transforming it into zeal for the evangelism of the world is a goal of conflict management within congregations. Internal conflict that endlessly spins its wheels in the mire of one's own rage simply becomes a destructive force. However, conflict can enable a person to rediscover her or his sense of passion and zeal for Christ's kingdom. Just as physical pain alerts us to problems within our bodies, so too does internal conflict focus attention on what really matters: the coming kingdom of Christ.

Conflict, as painful and malignant as it can sometimes be among human beings, is still under the control of almighty God. Congregational conflict cannot stop Christ's kingdom from coming. Jesus Christ is Lord of the church and he is its Messiah. When conflict strikes, it is Jesus' redemption and protection that help us to face it and to courageously work through it.

An ongoing venture

There is one phase remaining for the congregation wishing to transform its ministry: the tend phase. Turning around the ministry of a corporate body of Christ is not a one-time shot but an ongoing process. The newly constructed vision for mission requires tending over the years to come. The next chapter spells out how to tend the work that has occurred.

Reflection questions

1. Under what circumstances do you personally have the most difficulty dealing with conflict?

2. Think of several conflict situations over the course of your life. How did you handle them? What worked successfully? What was unsuccessful?

3. How has your congregation handled conflict in the past? In the present? How might the conflict transformation skills of your congregation be improved?

Notes

1. Edwin H. Friedman, *Generation to Generation: Family Process in Church and Synagogue* (New York: The Guilford Press, 1985), 23.

2. H. Newton Malony, *Win-Win Relationships: Nine Strategies For Settling Personal Conflicts Without Waging War* (Nashville: Broadman & Holman Publishers, 1995), 9.

3. Ibid., xi.

4. David W. Augsburger (unpublished lecture, Fuller Theological Seminary, Pasadena, Calif., February 1997).

5. Edward G. Dobson, Speed B. Leas, and Marshall Shelley, *Mastering Conflict and Controversy* (Portland, Ore.: Multnomah Press, 1992), 93.

6. Gordon W. Allport and Leo Postman, *The Psychology of Rumor* (New York: Henry Holt and Company, 1947).

7. Ibid., ix.

8. Ibid., 5.

9. Ibid., 2.

10. Kurt Lewin, *Resolving Social Conflicts: Selected Papers on Group Dynamics* (New York: Harper, 1948).

11. Kenneth C. Haugk, *Antagonists in the Church: How to Identify and Deal with Destructive Conflict* (Minneapolis: Augsburg Publishing House, 1988), 21–22.

10 Turning toward Health: Tend
Tending the Vision

Tend to God's vision as to a splendid garden: with faith, hope, and love.

Steven J. Goodwin

Submarines first became a part of the U.S. Navy in 1900. Though the Civil War's Monitor and Merrimac were the very earliest of submersibles, the first practical and serviceable vessels weren't in operation until the turn of the century. Even so, the submarine was still a crude ship that had limited capabilities while submerged. The small size of the earliest submarines did not allow much room for weapons, let alone food or fuel. Given all these limitations, the early submarines operated from shore stations, never straying too far from land.

In an effort to extend their range, submarines soon were attended to by a mother ship. The mother ship supplied what the submarine did not have space to carry. These auxiliary supply ships garnered the name of "tender" as they tended to the needs of the submarine and its crew.

World War II ushered in the era of the submarine. With it, specialized ships were designed and built specifically for the purpose of supporting the mission of the submarine. Submarines could now roam all around the globe wherever they were needed. Tender ships, with their technicians, repair crews, and medical and dental facilities, could resupply up to four submarines at a time. Though they are not the stuff of John Wayne movies, tender ships have played a very significant role in military might around the world in the past 50 years.

Just as submarines require the ongoing services of a specialized ship to tend to their needs, so too does the congregation require a continual tending to its renewed vision for mission. The vision will require frequent attention for it to remain a vital and active force for renewal of the congregation.

The final phase of the turn-around process is to tend the vision for mission. Just as a submarine cannot go too far from port without the support of a tender ship, the turn-around process will not last long without ongoing attention.

There are four aspects to the tend phase. These four stages are vital to maximizing all the work that has gone before. The stages of the tend phase are integrate, eliminate, evaluate, and celebrate. It falls to the elected governing body of the congregation to focus its ministries around these central tasks.

Integrate

"Integrate the vision everywhere." This maxim is the rallying cry for this first aspect of the tend phase. The new vision for mission cannot be seen as a sidelight nor can it become a cute slogan for doing the same old thing. A turn around requires fundamental change, which the new vision seeks to summarize. Even the term *turn around* implies the congregation is wholly changing direction. By definition this means that radical changes will occur. The vision runs through the center of everything the congregation seeks to accomplish. It is essential that the vision be wholly integrated into every aspect of congregational life.

The new vision will undoubtedly spur the introduction of new ministries to the life of the congregation. Integrating the vision into these emerging ministries is a matter of diligent focus. Each new ministry or programmatic outreach should be well conceptualized in advance with the vision in mind. Goals and objectives serve the larger vision and enable the new undertaking to be readily evaluated for its effectiveness in moving the congregation ahead toward its preferred future.

Integrating the vision into already-existing ministries is something else altogether. Courage and singleness of purpose are the essential elements needed to align even the most successful long-term ministries of the congregation with fresh vision for mission. While difficult, this can prove quite fruitful. Every master gardener knows that pruning a bush appears harsh at the time but incites the plant to become fuller and healthier. So also with existing ministries pruned to match the vision: they will blossom anew as they are given specific goals and objectives that are aligned with all the other ministries of the congregation.

Integrating the vision everywhere means that the congregation will, from this point onward, use the vision as its criteria for decision making. Will a proposed new ministry advance the vision or will it detract? Is staff time working for or against the vision? Is the congregation unified as it moves toward the same compass bearing? Where shall staff, ministry, and space be added, and for what purpose? These are just a sampling of the decisions made with the vision foremost in mind.

The difficulty lies in the universal phenomenon that the human mind is forgetful. Forgetfulness is not simply a natural by-product of the aging process; rather, forgetfulness serves the mind. Forgetting is the way the mind "dates" its memories. Fuzzy memories are far off or less remarkable, while events more recent or significant are remembered clearly. In this way, the mind sorts out which memories are recent or are long distant, which memories made a lasting impression and which are discardable. Understanding this biological fact serves the leadership by releasing each person from the personal guilt felt for being forgetful and setting each one free to continuously focus on the vision.

Rick Warren, pastor of Saddleback Valley Community Church, in his book *The Purpose Driven Church*, advocates what he calls the "Nehemiah Principle: Vision and purpose must be restated every twenty-six days to keep the church moving in the right direction."[1] This is his personal way of remembering to communicate the vision of Saddleback Church every month. Why? Because humans naturally forget and the vision must be continually kept as current memory.

To keep the memory of the vision alive, congregations need "vision keepers." Vision keepers are individuals who have the gift of focus and discernment, individuals who can gently but forcefully ask the important questions of priority. Does this serve our vision? Is this important enough to do? Will this make a difference? Vision keepers are those individuals Stephen Covey calls effective people: they "Begin with the end in mind" and they "Put first things first."[2]

Vision keepers are like the prophets of old. The job of the prophet is to continually call God's people back to what is central, to what is God's will. Vision keepers may be young or old, male or female, as the prophet Joel proclaimed on behalf of God: "I will pour out my spirit on all flesh; your sons and your daughters shall prophesy, your old men shall dream dreams, and your young men shall see visions. Even on the male and female slaves, in those days, I will pour out my spirit" (Joel 2:28).

While vision keepers may come from anywhere within the ranks of the congregation, the pastor of the congregation is among the keepers of God's vision. Faithfully listening for God and interpreting God's word is the central task of ordained ministry. The pastor is the congregation's most identifiable vision keeper. The congregation's pastor must also integrate the vision, given to the whole people of God, into the preaching and teaching life of the church. For congregations with more than one pastor, this responsibility may primarily lie with the lead or senior pastor.

Perhaps the most fruitful and long-lasting means of integrating the vision is to encourage dreaming. This can be done in fifteen minutes at the outset of a board meeting, in visitations with members, or in one-day summit meetings of the whole congregation. Whatever the setting, the people of God are invited to articulate the mental picture of the congregation's desired future. As they speak of their dreams for the future, the Holy Spirit has a way of lifting up the hearts and spirits of those present, encouraging them to dream also. In this manner, God's will spreads from mouth to ear throughout the membership.

Eliminate

Like a ship in dry-dock, the congregation will undoubtedly need to remove the barnacles of long-standing programs or ministries that are no longer effective. This is a difficult, even painful process. Many programs, while still producing good results, have long since lost sight of their goals. They may be worthy programs but are, quite honestly, not advancing the gospel. Many a congregation has come to look like a wonderful grassroots community social-service agency instead of a life-saving station for the rescue of souls. Programs are justified as an "outreach to the community," and may in fact be so, but are never evaluated for their effectiveness in touching the souls of their neighbors.

A plateaued or declining congregation, almost by definition, has very limited energy. It cannot do everything. It may not even be able to maintain what it was doing prior to the turn-around process and still undertake its newfound direction. Existing ministries that do not advance the vision for mission are best celebrated and then ended.

Bringing a program or ministry to an end is not a defeat. Letting an outmoded program die a graceful death is the supreme act of faith, for we know that God will raise a harvest in its place. The church need not fear failure; rather, the church is called to trust in God who has a plan for creation.

Evaluate

W. Edwards Deming and the Total Quality Management movement have instilled into today's business community the need for continual improvement as a means to excellence. Here the church can learn a new dance step from lay members who are business people. Continual improvement in the life of a congregation can be achieved through regular and honest evaluation. Such honesty reveals that it is precisely the lack of an evaluative process that allows congregations to continue ministries that no longer advance the kingdom. Frequent evaluation of a congregation's health alerts the membership long before its survival is at stake.

Evaluative criteria are best established upon the introduction of the new program. This is true also with the entire five-phased turn-around process. The vision team has identified two to three specific goals for each mission strategy. The task force charged with implementation of the strategy supports those goals with objectives. Both the goals and objectives need to be measurable and time-specific.

Fuzzy, unwritten goals and objectives are a common plague. Another widespread ailment is constructing too many goals. This dilutes the ability to focus the limited energies of the congregation. More than five goals is unworkable; three clearly written goals are ideal for each ministry of the congregation.

Involving the congregation in evaluation is just as important as involving members in the vision-building process. Turn-around congregations should plan one-day congregational summits one, three, and five years after the initiation of the act phase. Day-long summits are excellent venues for renewing commitment to the vision or adjusting it to meet changing circumstances. The collective wisdom and discernment of the body of Christ can then be used to evaluate the health condition of the congregation, much like a physician does during an annual physical.

Celebrate

Announcing to the community the changes taking place is the last stage of the tend phase. This announcement is important to a turn-around congregation because an unknown number of neighbors have decided against the congregation for one reason or another. Like it or not, the surrounding community develops a perception of the congregation through personal interactions, word of mouth, or community reputation. In the case of a plateaued or declining congregation it can be assumed that this perception is negative. Negative perceptions are barriers to be hurdled before the congregation can expect to be revitalized. Unchurched neighbors need a reason to give the spiritual life offered by the congregation another try.

For example, think of the local business that closed after doing poorly. Soon after changing ownership a familiar sign can usually be found proclaiming, "Under new management." Or think of the common household product that entices consumers to try it again by advertising in bold-face letters, "New and improved!" These efforts are attempts to garner the attention of people who long ago dismissed it to give the business or product another try. The turn-around church is in the same situation. The question is this: How does a congregation attract the attention of folks who have already decided that its ministry does not connect with their lives?

While the church does not want to adopt wholesale the tactics of Madison Avenue marketers, it can learn from them. Certainly Jesus Christ is the same "management" as before; even so, the congregation needs to communicate to the community that something has changed. The course of the congregation has been adjusted. This warrants another look by those who have long dismissed the life-giving ministries of Christ's people.

This should not be done, however, without first understanding exactly what the congregation hopes these new visitors will experience. If they give the congregation another try and their experience is the same as before, the results will be even more devastating than in the past. The negative perception has just been reinforced and set in concrete! It's wise to devise a means of surveying these negative perceptions beforehand. With this vital information, a turn-around congregation sets forth to change whatever it can, understanding that it cannot change the natural offense of the gospel or sugarcoat the word of God—some folks will always find objections to the Christian faith. Then the congregation can invite these people to give the church another look.

Many people love to give of themselves when they believe it makes a difference and there is a reasonable chance of success. A congregation's renewed vision is an opportunity to write an exciting new chapter in the history of the congregation and the community. Traditional newspaper advertisements, flyers in the local weekly paper, and door-to-door calling are ways to invite new people to become part of these exciting changes.

Congregations should prepare in advance an incorporation plan to disciple new members and involve them in ministry. Remember, this was exactly what Jesus did with the disciples. They had very little training before he sent them two-by-two with instructions to "cure the sick, raise the dead, cleanse the lepers, cast out demons" (Matthew 10:8).

Celebrations are a vital part of the tend phase. Turn-around congregations should plan special celebrations to lift up congregational milestones. Such celebrations are not just occasions for a party but serve to reinforce congregational motivation and the source of the congregation's renewed life. They are a time to give thanks and praise to the Lord of the church who makes all things possible. They are a time to recognize fellowship, unity, and joy in Christ. Remember the days of stagnation and decline? Remember the negative energy running throughout the membership? Celebrations reverse this energy drain. They reverberate throughout the community as the neighborhood buzzes with question, "What wonderful things are going on over at that church?"

The final result

Not all miracles are large. A turn around in the life of a Christian congregation does not mean that in every case the membership will increase a hundredfold. Many of God's miracles are unseen and are not acknowledged as such. It is more than justifiable to use the label "successful turn-around congregation" to describe the church that has returned to health, enthused its worship life with new energy, and once again become inviting to the community. Such a scenario is a miracle. It brings glory to God and draws the attention of unchurched people who begin to wonder about such a God who raises dead churches. "Could he resurrect my dead life too?" they ask.

The congregation undertaking this endeavor of reformation and turn around must prepare also for a less desirable outcome. The very real possibility exists that, after following all the steps outlined in this book and after a year or two of tending the vision, the congregation's decline continues unabated. Should this be the case, then God calls the remaining members to the ultimate act of faith: disband the congregation in order to give life to another mission somewhere else.

Imagine what might happen if a congregation were to praise God and close the doors in order to sell its assets and plant a new mission in some other locale. This is the supreme act of faith in a God of death and resurrection. What witness! What courage! Dying with grace and dignity is anything but defeat; it is a vision in itself.

Tending to God's business

From God we spring and to God we spend ourselves, tending to God's vision for our lives. This is what the Christian faith is all about. This is the business of Christ's church. We are called to tend to the business of death and resurrection as God reconciles the world to God.

Reflection questions

1. Identify God-given "prophets" within your congregation. How could you invite them to serve as the congregation's vision keepers?

2. What programs can be eliminated because they no longer support the vision? Which need to be retooled?

3. In what ways can your congregation attract the attention of your neighbors who long ago decided against your ministry?

Notes

1. Warren, *Purpose Driven Church*, 111.
2. Covey, *Seven Habits of Highly Effective People*, 95, 145.

Bibliography

Augsburger, David. *Caring Enough to Confront.* Glendale, Calif.: Gospel Light Publishing, 1981. This excellent volume helps to form a biblical and theological framework for dealing with conflict. Augsburger analyzes the conflict style of Jesus himself.

Barna, George. *The Power of Vision.* Ventura, Calif.: Regal Books, 1992. Barna offers helpful discussion about vision in this brief work. His perspective is optimistic and tends to discount the power of evil. The book fails to discuss how to get group ownership for a shared vision.

———. *Turnaround Churches: How to Overcome Barriers to Growth and Bring New Life to an Established Church.* Ventura, Calif.: Regal Books, 1993. This book offers a wide range of qualitative research on thirty successful congregational turn arounds. It is especially helpful to congregations that are considering calling a turn-around pastor as well as to pastors who seek to lead a congregational turn around.

Brandt, Donald M. *Worship and Outreach: New Services for New People.* Minneapolis: Augsburg Fortress, 1994. Adding a worship service of a different style can be an effective way to reach people who have not participated in church life. This practical resource provides church leaders with a process for planning a new service.

Callahan, Kennon L. *Twelve Keys to an Effective Church: Strategic Planning for Mission.* San Francisco: Harper & Row, 1983. This exceptional work has aided thousands of congregations around the world. Callahan offers a superior tool to assess the congregation.

Covey, Stephen R. *The Seven Habits of Highly Effective People: Restoring the Character Ethic.* New York: Simon & Schuster, 1989. This best-selling business book is a must-read for any congregational leader. Covey's principles readily translate to the context of Christian congregations.

Dethmer, Jim. Advanced Small Groups Tape Series. Pasadena, Calif.: Fuller Institute of Evangelism and Church Growth, 1994. This videocassette series details the steps for creating a network of small groups within your congregation. Video format allows church leaders to not only learn themselves but also to use these tapes to train small-group leaders.

George, Carl. *How to Break Growth Barriers: Capturing Overlooked Opportunities for Church Growth.* Grand Rapids, Mich.: Baker Book House, 1993. This book follows a vein similar to Larry Greiner's analysis of the stages of organizational growth. This book draws readers into deeper and more systematic thinking about barriers to congregational growth.

Greiner, Larry. "Evolution and Revolution as Organizations Grow." *Harvard Business Review* 50, no. 4 (July–August 1972): 37–46. This landmark paper remains one of *Harvard Business Review's* most popular reprints.

Haugk, Kenneth. *Antagonists in the Church: How to Identify and Deal with Destructive Conflict.* Minneapolis: Augsburg Publishing House, 1988.

Haugk offers a masterful analysis of antagonists, along with an excellent perspective on dealing with them.

Johnson, George S., David Mayer, and Nancy Vogel. *Starting Small Groups—and Keeping Them Going.* Minneapolis: Augsburg Fortress, 1995. Small groups are an effective way to build community within a congregation. This resource is a comprehensive guide for organizing, implementing, and growing congregational small-group ministry. Includes material for training small-group leaders.

Kouzes, James M. and Barry Z. Posner. *The Leadership Challenge: How to Keep Getting Extraordinary Things Done in Organizations.* San Francisco: Jossey-Bass Publishers, 1995. This popular book from the business world is worth reading for instruction in all the areas where one might be called to lead.

Malphurs, Aubrey. *Vision for Ministry in the 21st Century: Six Steps to Building Vision.* Grand Rapids, Mich.: Baker Books, 1992. Malphurs offers a comprehensive strategy for arriving at a compelling congregational vision for ministry.

Poling-Goldenne, David, project manager. *Making Christ Known: A Guide to Evangelism for Congregations.* Minneapolis: Augsburg Fortress, 1996. This is a practical resource for congregational task forces. Four areas of congregational evangelism activities are highlighted with ideas and additional resources identified for each area: hospitality and response, discipleship and incorporation, intentional community outreach, and communication and public relations.

Regele, Mike, with Mark Schulz. *Death of the Church.* Grand Rapids, Mich.: Zondervan Publishing House, 1995. Regele and Schulz have written a provocative book that they hope will motivate the church to recognize it's crisis and act quickly. They lay out the changes rocking our world and the life-or-death issues facing the church as a result.

Rothaar, Michael. *Counting Your Community: Using Census Statistics as Part of Congregational Planning.* Chicago: Evangelical Lutheran Church in America, 1996. Videocassette. This video resource will help congregational members discuss and interpret census data from their community. This information is vital to the study phase of a congregational turnaround.

Schaller, Lyle E. *44 Ways Up Off the Plateau.* Nashville: Abingdon Press, 1993. This book contains ideas to get thinking started. Schaller's "44 ways" will stimulate the creation of ideas to move beyond a congregation's current size. Schaller's work is grounded by his decades of work with thousands of congregations.

———. *Strategies for Change.* Nashville: Abingdon Press, 1993. This book is most helpful in provoking careful and thorough thought about what change will mean to a congregation. Most people only consider the initial elements of introducing change. Schaller encourages thinking about "Who decides?" and "Who has the authority?"

Schwarz, Christian. *Natural Church Development.* Carol Stream, Ill.: ChurchSmart Resources, 1996. Schwarz has done comprehensive research on the characteristics of healthy churches. This book will help leaders diagnose the congregation's weakest point, based on the findings of this study.

Steinke, Peter. *Healthy Congregations: A Systems Approach.* Bethesda, Md.: Alban Institute, 1996. This book is more theoretical than Schwarz's *Natural Church Development,* which is more statistical. In addition to this book, Steinke has developed two other important resources for the church: "BridgeBuilder Ministry" is a training program for working with churches in trouble and "Healthy Congregations" is a training program for lay leaders in congregations.

Strobel, Lee. *Inside the Mind of Unchurched Harry and Mary: How to Reach Friends and Family Who Avoid God and the Church.* Grand Rapids, Mich.: Zondervan, 1993. Strobel, through his groundbreaking work at Willow Creek Community Church in South Barrington, Illinois, has accurately assessed U.S. culture of unchurched people, allowing the reader to peek into the world outside of a faith perspective.

Weems, Lovett H. Jr. *Church Leadership: Vision, Team, Culture, and Integrity.* Nashville: Abingdon Press, 1993. Weems is a seminary president with extensive leadership experience. This book is thought provoking yet practical to the congregation wishing to turn things around.

Other resources

Percept Group, Inc., 151 Kalmus Dr., Ste. A104, Costa Mesa, CA 92626. 714-957-1282 or 800-442-6277 or fax 714-957-1924. Its Web site is at www.perceptnet.com. Percept Group offers detailed ministry-area profiles and other demographic data specific to a congregation.

Visions Decisions, PO Box 94144, Atlanta, GA 30377. 800-524-1445. Visions Decisions is another source of community demographic information for churches. They offer four types of reports, including a local population study with four versions—total population, African American, Asian American, and Hispanic American.